Splendid Occasions in English History, 1520–1947

In thys the ffyrst Rolle declaryng the Nombre of the kyngs Maiesties owne Shyppes Wich are Shypps and Shyppes Haven Wth theyr Tunnage and Nombre of men As Also the Ordenaunce Artillary & Munitions and Habillment for Warre ffor the Armyng and deffence of every of the sayd Shypps Agaynst theyr enemyes Vppon the See.

What ys To Saye

Men
Souldiours ... cccxlix
marynars ... ccc
Gonners ... l

For the Harry Grace à Dieu.
Ordenaunce Artillary Munitions Habillments for the Warre for the Armyng And in the deffence of the sayd Shypps

	Gonnes of Brasse	Gonnes of yron	Gonnepowder	Shotte of yron and leade	Shotte of Stoen	Bowes Bowestrynge Arrowes Morryspickes Byllys Dartes for toppys	Municions	Habillments for

SPLENDID OCCASIONS
IN ENGLISH HISTORY
1520~1947

by Ifan Kyrle Fletcher

with 12 colour and 66 monochrome reproductions

Cassell and Company Limited, London

CASSELL & COMPANY LTD.

37/38, St. Andrew's Hill, Queen Victoria Street, London, E.C.4

and at

210 Queen Street, Melbourne
P.O. Box 9, Wellington, N.Z.
P.O. Box 275, Cape Town
122 East 55th Street, New York
Islands Brygge 5, Copenhagen
Rua Maestro Elias Lobo 90, São Paulo

34 Clarence Street, Sydney
263/7 Adelaide Street West, Toronto
P.O. Box 1386, Salisbury, S. Rhodesia
15 Graham Road, Ballard Estate, Bombay, 1
Gartenstrasse 53, Düsseldorf
P.O. Box 959, Accra, Gold Coast

First published 1951

SET IN 14PT BEMBO TYPE AND PRINTED IN GREAT BRITAIN
BY W. S. COWELL LTD, AT THE BUTTER MARKET, IPSWICH

TO

His Grace The DUKE OF NORFOLK, K.G.

in whom is vested

by the Crown

by virtue of his hereditary office of

EARL MARSHAL OF ENGLAND

the ordering of all State ceremonial

THIS BOOK

is respectfully dedicated

List of Occasions and Reproductions

	Page
The Great Harry (*Colour plate*)	*Frontispiece*

From *A Declaration of the Royal Navy of England composed by Anthony Anthony, 1546*, in the Pepysian Library, Magdalene College, Cambridge. Reproduced by courtesy of the Master and Fellows of Magdalene College.

	Page
THE FIELD OF THE CLOTH OF GOLD, 1520	1
The Embarkation of Henry VIII at Dover	5
The Field of the Cloth of Gold	6
The Meeting of Henry VIII and François I	8
Henry VIII. Medallion Portrait	8
François I. Medallion Portrait	8
THE PROGRESSES OF QUEEN ELIZABETH, 1558–1603	11
Queen Elizabeth on her Way to the Wedding of Anne Russell and Lord Herbert at Blackfriars (*Colour plate*)	10
Queen Elizabeth proceeding to Parliament	15
Queen Elizabeth's Procession to her Coronation	15
A Yeoman of the Guard attending Queen Elizabeth on a Progress	17
Queen Elizabeth's Seal	17
George Gascoigne presenting his Book 'The Tale of Hemetes the Hermyte pronownced before the Q. Majesty at Woodstocke, 1575'	17
Queen Elizabeth's Entertainment by the Earl of Hertford at Elvetham, 1591	19
THE WEDDING OF PRINCESS ELIZABETH AND COUNT FREDERICK, 1613	21
A Section from a Vellum Roll of the Processions and Tournament at Heidelberg (*Colour plate*)	20
Frederick, the Elector Palatine	25
Engraving symbolizing the Marriage of Princess Elizabeth and the Elector Palatine	25

	Page
Elizabeth of Bohemia	25
The Procession of Princess Elizabeth and Frederick to Chapel Royal, 14 February 1613	26
Frederick greeting Elizabeth outside Heidelberg	29
A Torchbearer in 'The Memorable Maske'	30
A Masker in 'The Lord's Maske'	30
A Page, like a Fiery Spirit, in 'The Lord's Maske'	30
The Elector Palatine leaving England with his Bride	31
The Duke of Wurtemberg	32
THE RESTORATION, CORONATION AND WEDDING OF CHARLES II, 1660–1–2	35
The Restoration of Charles II (*Colour plate*)	34
Charles II's Arrival at The Hague	39
The Ball given to Charles II at The Hague on his Departure	40
The Arrival of the Prince de Ligne at the Tower of London	43
The Prince de Ligne presenting his Son to Charles II at Whitehall	44
Charles II in his Coronation Robes	45
Catherine of Braganza	46
The Departure of Catherine from Lisbon	47
Catherine's Arrival at London	47
THE CREATION OF THE MOST HONOURABLE ORDER OF THE BATH, 1725	49
The Procession of the Order of the Bath	48
Prince William offering his Sword to the Dean	53
The Knights at Dinner	55
A Knight's Collar and a Knight's Star	56
Medal of Prince William in the Robes of a Knight of the Bath	57

LIST OF OCCASIONS AND REPRODUCTIONS

Page

THE SHAKESPEARE JUBILEE, STRATFORD-ON-AVON,
1769   59

    The Scene at the High Cross (*Colour plate*)   58

    The Statue of Shakespeare at the Town Hall   62

    James Boswell in the Dress of an armed Corsican Chief   63

    A Printed Cotton Handkerchief with Scenes relating to the Jubilee   64

    Garrick reciting the Ode   67

    View of the Amphitheatre and Firework Screen   68

    Garrick as Steward of the Jubilee   69

THE CORONATION OF GEORGE IV, 1821   71

    King George IV and his Train-bearers (*Colour plate*)   70

    The Procession from Westminster Hall to the Abbey   75

    The Archbishop of Canterbury placing the Crown on the King's Head   76

    Stephanoff's Drawings of People Present at the Coronation   79

    The King's Champion in the Banqueting Hall   80

THE FUNERALS OF NELSON, 1806, AND
WELLINGTON, 1852   83

    Nelson's Funeral Procession from Greenwich to Whitehall (*Colour plate*)   82

    The Funeral Procession of Lord Nelson from the Admiralty to St Paul's   87

    The Interment of the Remains of Lord Nelson at St Paul's   88

    Lord Nelson's Funeral Car   89

    The Duke of Wellington's Funeral Car   89

    Wellington's Funeral Procession passing Apsley House (*Colour plate*)   90

    An Impression of Wellington's Funeral Car passing Buckingham Palace   92

    The Departure from the Horse Guards   93

    The Duke of Wellington's Lying-in-State at Chelsea Hospital   94

    The Ceremony at St Paul's   94

THE VISIT OF LOUIS-PHILIPPE, KING OF THE FRENCH,
TO QUEEN VICTORIA, 1844   97

    Le Débarquement à Portsmouth (*Colour plate*)   96

    Intérieur du Carosse de la Reine   101

    The Arrival of Louis-Philippe at Windsor   102

    The Reception of Louis-Philippe   105

    The Departure from Gosport in a Storm   106

THE OPENING OF THE GREAT EXHIBITION, 1851   109

    The Crystal Palace (*Colour plate*)   108

    1851: The First of May   113

    The Grand Entrance to the Great Exhibition   114

    The Opening of the Great Exhibition   117

    The Great Exhibition from the Serpentine   118

THE WEDDING OF THE PRINCE OF WALES AND
PRINCESS ALEXANDRA, 1863   121

    H.R.H. The Princess Alexandra Caroline of Denmark in her Wedding Dress and H.R.H. Albert Edward, Prince of Wales (*Colour plate*)   120

    Princess Alexandra arriving at the Bricklayers Arms Station   125

    A Visit to Eton School   126

    The Bridesmaids   129

    The Signing of the Marriage Attestation   130

THE WEDDING OF PRINCESS ELIZABETH AND PRINCE
PHILIP, THE DUKE OF EDINBURGH, 1947   133

    The Design for Princess Elizabeth's Wedding Dress (*Colour plate*)   132

    Princess Elizabeth and the Duke of Edinburgh   136

    The Scene inside the Abbey   137

ACKNOWLEDGEMENTS

The preparation of this book would have been impossible without assistance from many scholars, librarians, museum officials, and others interested in the history of ceremonial, who have generously placed their knowledge at my disposal. The Royal collections at Windsor Castle, Buckingham Palace, and St James's Palace have been a constant source of inspiration. For the opportunity to examine them and for permission to adapt the binding of George III's copy of Angelo's *Ecole des Armes*, 1763, for the binding of this book, I tender my respectful thanks to His Majesty the King. The sources to whom I am indebted for the illustrations I have recorded on the pages where the reproductions appear.

I cannot allow this opportunity to pass without recording my debt to my wife and a group of intimate friends, who by relieving me of other duties, enabled me to write this book, and I trust that all the others who have allowed me to make calls on their time and patience will accept this as an expression of my sincere gratitude.

My special thanks are due to the following:

C. K. Adams

Otto Andrup

Eric Bligh

Alan Brock

Lieut-General Sir Frederick Browning, K.B.E., C.B., D.S.O.

Miss Muriel St Clare Byrne

Sir Fitzroy H. A. G. Calthorpe, Bart, C.B.E.

Mrs James Carruthers, C.H.

Edward Croft Murray

G. S. Dugdale

Miss Dorothy Dymond, O.B.E.

H. Granville Fell

Levi Fox

Mademoiselle Gauchery

Monsieur M. Grenier

J. D. Heaton-Armstrong, M.V.O., Chester Herald

Martin R. Holmes, F.S.A.

C. P. Humphery

Dr R. W. Ladborough

Mademoiselle R. M. Langlois

James Laver

The Princess de Ligne

Monsieur Mauricheau-Beaupré

Oliver Millar

Sir Owen Morshead, K.C.V.O.

James C. Palmes

Mrs Ann Price

Dr Oskar Regele

M. S. Robinson

The Marquis of Salisbury

Bertram Shuttleworth

Sacheverell Sitwell

Francis Thompson, F.S.A.

Monsieur Jean Vallery-Radot

Introduction

CELEBRATION HAS ALWAYS been in the hearts of men. It reveals itself in an impulse older than recorded story and emerging at all times in the four quarters of the world. The temple dancers of Angkor and the horn dancers of Abbots Bromley, Peruvian priests celebrating the sun-feast and Roman priests officiating at the Eucharist, the knights of primitive Europe raising their king upon a shield and binding a silken diadem about his head, and the crowds gathering in the Mall to watch the Coronation procession drive to Westminster Abbey—all these expressed—and still express—the need to celebrate, to observe with ritual the intimately entwined traditions of war and kingship, religion and pleasure. The acts of celebration seem to divide themselves into the primitive festivals associated with fertility and triumph, and the religious festivals extending from ancestor worship to Christianity. But no guide to the elemental nature of these rites will do anything but confuse if it attempts to simplify these complex and interwoven traditions. As they emerge into the comparative daylight of the last thousand years, they are clearer to see but are still only suggestive to the understanding. Gloriously stimulated by the arts, they have penetrated the whole area of public life, so that those who saw a marriage festivity costumed and designed by Leonardo or a triumphal entry planned by Dürer, who listened in royal company to a masque set to music by Lawes or heard the drumming of the feet of courtly dancers, knew that the great moments of our civilized life were being celebrated with splendour. But behind the silken hangings, the gilded chariots, the web of sound and the metre of the dance, only a few may have been dimly aware of the old enchantment.

At the moment when celebration was glittering with all the arts of the Renaissance, its inner enemies arose—those who saw in it nothing but luxury and extravagance, who accused it of tending to frivolity and carelessness, who went about, in the name of morality, to crush this gay flower of pleasure. Francis Bacon, himself one of the devisers of a sumptuous masque for the wedding of Princess Elizabeth, could yet write, 'these things are but toys, to come amongst such serious Observation.' The instinct to celebrate constantly asserts itself afresh, but after three centuries of such divisions in the minds of men, its links with some of the most ancient impulses are sadly weakened. It is not easy to know whether the decay of celebration is to be more regretted than some of the attempts to revive it without tradition, for amusement only, like a vivid bed of rootless flowers, doomed to fade overnight. Even our Machine Age has its occasions which demand commemoration with splendour. They can be profoundly satisfying only in so far as they bear within themselves, no matter what form they take for the people of their day, the hints of strange and immemorial ceremonies. In Britain the links still hold, though worn perilously thin in places. While they hold, let us examine them, sharing, for a moment and at a great distance, some of the pleasure of our ancestors in the events they found significant, the ceremonies they used to celebrate them, and the traces they preserved of the ancient magic.

Splendid Occasions is a brief record in words and pictures of certain moments in English history when the event, in its celebration, seems to carry a banner emblematic of its time and mood. The occasions are chosen from four of the many paths into which the elemental pageant of festivity has divided itself. Pre-eminent amongst these are regal ceremonies—coronations, royal weddings, royal interviews and state entries. Linked to these by long tradition if not by original foundation are the solemnities of chivalry. Less closely connected, but still deriving some of their dignity from association with the king, are events honouring the illustrious men of our race, here represented by the contrast of the state funerals of Nelson and Wellington. One occasion only is quite free from royal influence, the first Shakespeare commemoration at Stratford-on-Avon. This was a junction of local patriotism and the arts, typical of the re-emergence of celebration in more democratic surroundings. The opening of the Great Exhibition marks the return of these utilitarian festivals to Royal patronage.

These events, selected not quite at random, are offered in the hope that they will be accepted as symbols of the rich procession of festivity with which English history is thronged. The coronations of Queen Elizabeth, Charles II, and George IV, each reflecting within the same ceremony the personality of the monarch and the atmosphere of the times, might have been matched by the stately coronation of James II. The King's religious leanings and his exalted conception of his office caused him to go minutely into the records of the past and to order a solemnity based upon tradition and rich in precedents, of which Francis Sandford, his chronicler, wrote, 'A Man cannot do Right to the Solemnity that is here in Question, without carrying his Thoughts back at the same time into the Boundless Antiquity.' The coronation of Edward VI, famous for its graceful cavalcade through London, held one strange feature from the mists of time. 'A native of Arragon' slid down a rope from the battlements of St Paul's before the King, climbed the rope again to the roof of the cathedral and there 'played certain mysteries on the said rope'. The presence of this Spanish acrobat at an English coronation introduces into a royal ceremony an element from the most ancient pagan festivals, the wild man, the green man, the tree spirit.

The royal weddings of Princess Elizabeth, daughter of James I; Charles II; Edward, Prince of Wales; and the recent celebration of Princess Elizabeth's marriage, afford the widest variety of interest. But the exclusion of the wedding of Prince Arthur to Catharine of Aragon in 1501 causes a pang of regret. Nothing in the history of English pageantry could have been finer than the procession that passed before the King and Queen in Westminster Hall—the great gilded cars in the shape of a castle, a ship, and a mountain, bearing 'goodly and fresh ladyes', children 'singing most sweetly and harmoniously', and 'fower great beastes with chaines of gold'. Of another sort was the uneasy magnificence of the summer day at Winchester when Mary I married Philip of Spain. The Spanish courtiers, elegant and dignified, moved through the suspicious glances of the little town, while the whole country seethed with insurrection. The mood of rejoicing is caught again in the records of royal entries and interviews. The meeting of Henry VIII and François I is unrivalled in its splendour, and the meeting of Queen Victoria and Louis-Philippe reaches the other zenith of plainness and simplicity. But neither the carnival glitter of the Field of the Cloth of Gold nor the informality of Victoria and Louis riding alone in Windsor Great Park could bring understanding between these two great nations. It is pleasanter to remember the warm welcome given by the Dutch to William III when he returned to his own country after the revolution of 1688, or the beautiful trappings erected to greet James VI of Scotland when he arrived in London to become James I of England. The superb baroque arches, built by Stephen Harrison, framed a procession that still delights the imagination. In Cheapside there was a summer arbour; in the Strand an invention of a rainbow, with the moon, sun and seven stars; and everywhere there were lovely boys and girls, dressed in white silk, making speeches of welcome, and singing 'heavenly music'. The whole vast theatrical pageant glowed in the streets of London for a day, and then evaporated, and became only a memory of what the mind and heart of man can do when they are stirred to celebrate.

The event selected to represent the splendour of chivalry is the pretended revival —but actually the creation—of the Order of the Bath by George I in 1725. This was a surprising medley of genuine and invented traditions, but it more than justifies its place by emphasizing that knighthood is now peculiar to the British Empire and that in its ceremonial is preserved the ritual of the accolade, in which the subject personally receives the honour at the hands of his sovereign. It is right to see the Order of the Bath in perspective against the most ancient and noble order now existing, the Order of the Garter. Here, if further evidence be needed, can be seen the gradual emerging of a great ceremonial from the courtly and warlike life of the Middle Ages, a process so rooted in the past that the exact date of foundation and the reason for the choice of emblem are now subjects of antiquarian argument. It is certain that the order was founded in the reign of Edward III, but the common tradition of the garter is dismissed by Heylyn as 'a vain and idle romance derogatory both to the founder and the order'. As the medieval conceptions of life have passed away there has been a tendency to see the chivalrous spirit as a class spirit, to belittle the fantastic courtesies it involved, and to blame it for encouraging the love of war. But the magnificent spectacle of the installation of a knight in St George's Chapel carries the beholders back to principles which were old in 1348 when Edward issued the first letters patent for the preparation of the royal chapel, and makes them participants in a ceremony which, with the accretions of time, still has elements leading into the dim recesses of Norman, Saxon and Teutonic customs.

The deeply felt occasions of public rejoicing and solemnity are often associated with praising famous men. England possesses a great tradition of impressive funeral ceremonies, from the pathetically beautiful *cortège* that brought the body of Sir Philip Sidney home from the Netherlands, the grim funeral of Cromwell, the stately interments of Monk and Marlborough, to the funerals here described—Nelson's, with an outburst of popular emotion rare in English history, and Wellington's, the apotheosis of the great commander. In 1769 David Garrick planned and carried through in spite of much ridicule and the worst vagaries of the English weather, a celebration of England's greatest son. The first Shakespeare commemoration at Stratford had none of the emotional appeal of a state funeral and it revealed certain absurd aspects, but it must be honourably remembered as the progenitor of many festivals of the arts which have since brought pleasure to millions. There are similarities in the Great Exhibition, an event which gathered up the ends of the earth, in all their wonderful strangeness, and domesticated them, with a royal blessing, in Hyde Park.

INTRODUCTION

These are the occasions. In the body of the book they stand isolated; here they are seen for a moment against their background. So placed, their quality as the toys of another age may seem to be worthy of a more tender regard than Bacon knew. As far back as man can look, they have stirred the heart with their appeal to eye and ear, the flash of colour, the swing of marching men, the thrilling peal of trumpets sending the birds fluttering into the sky, perfumed nosegays in the ballroom, the last rocket dropping into a lake as cloudy as a cat's eyes moist with sleep, the quiet music of ancient instruments playing beneath a golden bough.

The Field of the Cloth of Gold

1520

'Twixt Guynes and Arde:
I was then present, saw them salute on horseback:
Beheld them, when they lighted, how they clung
In their embracement, as they grew together:

SHAKESPEARE, King Henry VIII
Act I, Scene i

The Field of the Cloth of Gold, 1520

AT THE END OF MAY in the year 1520 the people of the towns and villages of Kent bordering the road from London to the coast, were living at the full stretch of excitement. Each day, through their narrow streets were passing heavy convoys of wagons, and teams of fine horses led by grooms in the liveries of the greatest nobles in the land, followed by the chariots of ladies with their lords riding at the side. For days these cavalcades went by, more than five thousand noblemen, ladies, chaplains and servants, with nearly two thousand horses, all thronging the roads to Dover to cross with their king to France. Henry VIII, still under thirty, still 'exceedingly fair, and as well proportioned as possible', still affable and benign', as the Venetian Ambassador described him, had decided to make a brilliant visit to Francis I. The way for this meeting had been opened two years before by the betrothal of the infant Princess Mary to the Dauphin. Since then there had been a bitter struggle between Francis and Charles, the King of Spain, for the Imperial throne left vacant by the death of Maximilian. Although Charles had been elected to succeed 'the last of the knights', his rival was powerful. Henry saw an opportunity to place England in a balancing position between these two great monarchs, and this train of horsemen, chariots and wagons pouring out of London was the first grasp of his hand to seize it.

On 21 May the King left his favourite palace, built on a terrace above the river at Greenwich, and rode towards Canterbury, there to celebrate the festival of Whitsun. With him were his Queen, Catharine of Aragon, his beautiful sister, Mary, the Dowager Queen of France, and her handsome and much-married husband, the Duke of Suffolk. They made the journey by easy stages, passing without haste in regal pageantry through towns and villages. In the centre of all eyes was the King, 'the arche Phenix', with his tawny beard. His sister and her husband matched him in their looks but his Queen, 'of low stature and rather stout', was more beloved by the people than any of them. For it was known that she regarded the treaty with France, the betrothal of her daughter to the Dauphin, and this extravagant visit to the French king, with dislike, as did all right-thinking Englishmen. She had tried to delay the departure by saying that she could not possibly have her dresses ready in less than three months. Perhaps it was owing to her influence as well as to the diplomacy of

Wolsey that immediately after their arrival, on the fourth day, at Canterbury, news came that the Emperor Charles, her nephew, had arrived off Hythe on his way from Spain to his dominions in the Netherlands.

Wolsey hastened to Dover to meet him. Charles was installed with great pomp in the Castle, but in the middle of the night he was roused by the news that the King was riding from Canterbury by torch-light to see him. They met, embraced and talked. They talked for four days. The Emperor could not have hoped to persuade Henry to cancel his visit to France at this late hour. What was the purpose of this plain, dignified young man, uneasy master of more than half Europe, in coming so far and so late, from his music, his birds, his mechanical toys, the simplicities he enjoyed, to talk with the King and the Cardinal? They found gluttony his only weakness, so they feasted him for six hours at a meal and then they rode with him towards his ships.

On Thursday, 31 May, the King, splendidly clad in a garment of cloth-of-gold edged with ermine, embarked at Dover. Some say that he used for the crossing the great ship *Henry Grace à Dieu*, always called *The Great Harry*. The King had seen to her plans himself, had watched with pride during the two years of her building, and now enjoyed the possession of the greatest ship afloat, in name a warship but to him one of his palaces, superbly fitted for entertainment, a worthy background to a royal banquet. The wind was favourable, the crossing was made in a few hours and at eleven in the morning Henry landed at the English port of Calais. Here he rested for four days while Francis I and his retinue arrived at the town of Ardres, twelve miles away, on the top of a hill. Many great noblemen rode from each camp to salute the kings. Above all of them was Cardinal Wolsey when, as the English king's ambassador, he rode to Ardres in ecclesiastical and secular state. The great Cross was borne before him and a company of noblemen, all in crimson velvet with gold chains, rode ahead, with servants leading mules bearing coffers of rich gifts, surrounded by a company of English archers. When they came to the gate of Ardres they found the steep, narrow street lined all the way to the royal lodgings by the French king's Swiss guard. Attended by the princes of France, and heralded by trumpets, Wolsey was conducted through the town to the pavilions set up on the bank of a little stream in the grounds of a ruined castle. Of these pavilions three were for the use of the King, in the centre of them a great 'house of solace and sport' made of rich blue cloth scattered with golden stars, the roof 'like the firmament'. Francis's private pavilion was made of gold brocade with three circular stripes of azure-coloured velvet ornamented with golden lilies in relief. At the summit of the tent was a golden statue of St Michael, standing on a great golden ball. From the feet of the statue darted twelve rays of the same azure velvet, extending thirty feet downwards. A shield richly emblazoned with the arms of France stood in an opening.

The King and the Cardinal debated for two days. When Francis saw the pomp with which Henry honoured his minister, and when he realized Wolsey's genius in the management of affairs, he placed in his hands complete responsibility for the details of the interview.

Early in the next week the English court moved to the grim little town of Guines, five miles nearer to Ardres but still in English territory. It was almost on the French border and possessed a powerful castle for its defence. For the occasion Henry transformed the appearance of the town by erecting a pleasure palace. Hundreds of workmen were sent from England to build the royal lodging. The framework of a wooden building three hundred and twenty-eight feet square and one hundred and twenty-eight feet high was made in London. It was placed near the castle at Guines and covered with canvas painted and gilt to represent the most sumptuous Roman ornaments. All the rooms had large windows so that a half of the wall-space was glass. Silk hangings of green and white, the colours of the House of Tudor, decorated the walls, and the ceilings were covered with white and gold silk embroidered with the Tudor rose. There were many audience chambers, all with cloths of estate, and a chapel with two royal closets. On the lawn before the great gateway was a marble fountain which, during the whole time of the interview, ran with hypocras, wine and water, and, at its head stood 'in letters of Romaine in gold' the invitation, *Faicte bonne chere qui vouldra*. Around the palace, the castle and the lawns were grouped eight hundred and twenty pavilions, the lodgings of the English visitors.

Henry's palace was the wonder of France. The noblemen in whose midst Leonardo da Vinci had lived until so recently and for whom he had designed such palaces as Amboise, confessed that nothing like it had been seen before. But its designers, while building it to delight the eyes of its beholders, had not forgotten other possibilities than pleasure. From the palace into the strong fortress of Guines was a gallery for the secret passage of the King's person, 'the more for the Kinges ease'. This gallery was disguised with foliage so that it became as difficult to find as the Castle of Dedalus

or the garden of Morgan le Fé. The same spirit of distrust was behind Wolsey's prolonged negotiations with Francis concerning the date and place of the meeting. For four days the two kings, with every evidence of their splendour and power gathered round them, remained only seven miles apart. They sent each other gay words of greeting, but in their minds were dark thoughts.

On the afternoon of Thursday, 7 June, King Henry set out from the castle of Guines. A gun was fired from the fortress as a signal of departure and an answering shot was heard from Ardres. At the head of the procession was the Royal Guard, followed by the squires, knights and barons. Then, riding alone, came the King, in a jewelled suit of silver damask and a plumed velvet cap. Behind him thronged the greatest noblemen of the realm, led by the Lord Cardinal. To the eye it was a brave procession, but as these horsemen rode up the long, gentle slope from Guines there were doubts in many hearts. Lord Abergavenny voiced them to the King. There was a halt. Discussion burst out amongst those within the royal circle. Murmurs and suspicions spread to the footmen in front, to the henchmen, to the archers gathered round. There was a pause, in which all eyes were turned to the King—and slowly the King rode forward.

At the top of the long low hill the English procession spread out and looked down into the Val d'Oré. It was a shallow valley, less than a mile wide and many miles long. From the two parallel ridges the road dropped steeply, sheltered by a few trees and protected by high banks. For the rest of the way it stretched like a taut ribbon across the bare plain. The Englishmen fanned out along the western ridge, hundreds of them, in cloth-of-gold, their banners streaming above them, their weapons flashing in the golden sunlight of late afternoon. And across the valley, drawn up on the eastern ridge, they saw a thousand Frenchmen, who, if they had but known it, were as doubtful as themselves. In the centre was their King, Francis I, in doublet and cloak of cloth-of-gold, his breast bare. He wore white boots and a black velvet cap with black feathers and flashing jewels. He was riding a magnificent black Spanish horse. From the French side too, came the sparkle of weapons, but one flash near the King was more brilliant than all the others. It was the great Sword of France held aloft by the Duc de Bourbon. The King spoke to the Marquis of Dorset and, with an answering flash, the English Sword of State was drawn. Then, to the music of trumpets, sackbuts and clarions, the two kings rode slowly down into the valley. When they were within a stone's throw of one another, they spurred their horses and, cap in hand, they embraced. The horses reared away but the sovereigns swung them together again and returned to the embrace.

THE EMBARKATION OF HENRY VIII AT DOVER

An Anonymous Painting at Hampton Court

Reproduced by gracious permission of His Majesty the King

THE FIELD OF THE CLOTH OF GOLD
An Anonymous Painting at Hampton Court
Reproduced by gracious permission of His Majesty the King

Then the kings dismounted and went, arm in arm, into a small and elegant pavilion which Henry had erected in the middle of the valley. The outside was covered with figured gold brocade and the interior was hung with tapestries embroidered in gold and silver. Here were set two chairs of state and the kings dined together with much mirth and good pleasure. Meanwhile, the French nobles flocked down into the valley and were served with excellent wine, which they gratefully drank because of the great heat and the general turmoil. But the English nobles were not yet at their ease. They remained withdrawn on the crest of the ridge, watching the proceedings from a distance, noticing how some of the French went 'slily masked' and judging them all as 'rufflers'. But when the kings had finished their banquet and came out into the cool evening light, there was great rejoicing and the cavalcades returned to their lodgings to the sweet, thin music of hautboys, fifes and clarions.

The kings had met at last, but this was only the beginning. They continued to meet daily for another seventeen days and while they feasted, tilted, wrestled and danced, the astute Wolsey was gauging how much the English favour was worth to the French king. On Saturday, 9 June, the jousting field was inspected. It was three hundred yards long and one hundred and six yards wide with stands for the spectators and a private box for the queens, adorned with tapestry and protected by glass screens. On this occasion the gracious ceremony took place of setting up two artificial bushes, hawthorn for Henry and raspberry for Francis. The branches were of cloth of gold, the flowers and fruit of silver and 'Venice gold'. On these were hung the royal shields and the articles of the jousts. On Sunday Francis rode to Guines to lunch with the Queen of England and Henry returned the visit later in the day, dining with the Queen of France at Ardres. After dinner there was music, at which King Henry was wonderfully proficient. It must have been for an occasion such as this that he composed his ballad, 'Passetyme with good cumpanye'. Meanwhile Francis was dancing at Guines and, so reported an Italian diplomat, 'part of the time he made love to the ladies there'.

Monday was an important day in the festivities. The royal ladies made their appearance in state for the first time. Catharine, the Queen of England; Claude, the Queen of France; and Henry's sister, Mary, the Dowager Queen of France, met at the jousting field. Mary, widowed while still a girl, had known both courts. To the French she was 'la Blanche Reine' and to her fell the task of persuading Catharine of Aragon to accept with grace this distasteful visit. The ways to the field of exercise were choked with chariots, litters and palfreys, all draped with cloth-of-gold and silver, embroidered with the arms and devices of these great ladies. The two queens met and, so far as the spectators could see, 'eyther saluted other right honorably'. Then they took their seats in the sumptuous box of honour and watched their husbands tilting. The monarchs' horses had exquisite trappings of symbolic significance. Thus Francis's courser was clothed in purple satin, brocaded with gold and embroidered with raven's wings in black, a conceit of gallantry, while Henry's had trappings of cloth-of-gold and russet velvet, designed to signify the lordship of the narrow sea. Each day the trappings of the horses were changed and each day the emblems had esoteric meanings. Alas! that so brave a show should have been marred by the weather. The spell of brilliant sunshine disappeared and a spring storm blew and rained for three days. Tilting took place on the next day, in spite of the rain, but on the thirteenth the gale was so severe that the kings were forced to abandon their sport and watched Englishmen and Bretons wrestling instead. It was this day that the weather brought a serious blow to the hospitable and pleasure-loving Francis. The gale increased in fury and swept down the pavilions which were the pride of his heart. For the remaining ten days of the meeting the French festivities took place in a house Francis had built at Ardres, which, though it had the advantage of being permanent, lacked the colour and elegance of his great pavilion.

The weather improved and for two more days they jousted. Henry was insatiable. He had with him in the lists six coursers, trapped with crimson velvet, all decorated with roses of beaten gold and little bells. He ran them for two hours each day, and all the time he laughed. On the second day he ran so freshly and so long that one of his best coursers was dead that night. But, in spite of the sport and the feasts, there was still a distance between the two monarchs. The King of France was hurt to find so little confidence growing between them. So one morning he rose much earlier than usual, took the first two gentlemen and the first page he found, mounted his horse and rode to Guines. Making his way among two hundred surprised archers he went to the King's chamber and woke him. Henry was dumbfounded but greeted him like a brother. He took from his neck a collar of Persian rubies, fastened with diamonds and pearls, and begged Francis to wear it. The French king took from his wrist a bracelet of precious stones and offered it to Henry for love of him. When they had both put on their tokens, Henry wished to get up and Francis told him he should have no valet but himself. So he warmed his vest and helped him to dress. Nothing could have been a bolder stroke to achieve intimacy; no one could have done it with a finer grace than Francis; no one could have received it with heartier friendship than Henry; but Wolsey was still debating whether the French king or the Roman emperor would be the better ally for England.

Top: THE MEETING OF HENRY VIII AND
FRANÇOIS I
Detail from bas-relief, Hôtel de Bourgtheroulde, Rouen
(Photograph: Bibliothèque des Monuments Historiques, Paris)
Crédit Industriel de Normandie, Rouen

Left: HENRY VIII
Medallion portrait in bas-relief, Hôtel de Bourgtheroulde, Rouen
Crédit Industriel de Normandie, Rouen

Right: FRANÇOIS I
Medallion portrait in bas-relief, Hôtel de Bourgtheroulde, Rouen
(Photograph: Bibliothèque des Monuments Historiques, Paris)
Crédit Industriel de Normandie, Rouen

The following week was spent in archery and wrestling. The use of the bow had become unfashionable in France, hence Henry's strong and accurate marksmanship caused much delight. His skill befitted a monarch who founded a Fraternity of St George for the practice of shooting. Even at wrestling this vigorous man could not be a spectator only but tried a fall with the French king. Yet as the week passed thoughts began to turn towards tangible results of this prodigious outlay of wealth, skill and taste. The two kings promised each other to build, at their common expense, a handsome palace in the valley and to visit each other there once a year. This might serve the ends of diplomacy and pleasure, but they thought too of their divine duty and laid the foundation stone of a church to be dedicated to Our Lady of Friendship. The outward purpose of the meeting had been to strengthen the treaty of peace made between the two nations in 1518. This intention was now solemnized at a High Mass sung by Cardinal Wolsey in the chapel in Henry's palace at Guines. It was an occasion of ecclesiastical pomp splendidly devised by the proud cardinal. The clergy wore vestments of gold tissue, powdered with red roses, each woven in a single piece by the finest craftsmen of Florence. They officiated at the High Altar on which stood twelve golden images under a canopy of cloth-of-gold embroidered with pearls. Gathered before them were the two kings, three ambassadors and the noblemen of both countries. The choral portions were sung alternately by the Chapels Royal of England and France. Henry's entire Chapel attended from England, under its famous master, William Cornyshe, and the singing men were led by the incomparable Dr Robert Fayrfax. A French nobleman recorded that the Mass was 'somptueusement chantée'. The Cardinal pronounced the Benediction. The peace was ratified and proclaimed by the heralds of both countries. But, at this very moment, it was whispered later by the superstitious, a great salamander, spouting fire, a portent of disaster, appeared over Ardres, flew towards Guines, passed the royal chapel and disappeared into the air.

The Field of the Cloth of Gold was drawing to an end. The next day was Sunday, 24 June, the Feast of St John and the crown of high summer. This great interview, arranged with such consummate skill, was to be brought to an appropriate conclusion. There were farewell festivities at Guines and Ardres. Francis dined *en masque*, with the Queen of England. Henry and his sister, Mary, also in masquing costume, rode to Ardres to dine with the Queen of France. They took with them William Cornyshe, in his capacity as Master of the Children of the Chapel Royal, an ingenious deviser of masques and pageants. To him fell the task of making an entertainment worthy to be offered by Henry to the Queen of France as a climax to this great occasion. The French ladies received the King with exquisite delicacy of feeling. They and all the court were dressed in black velvet, as though in mourning, and over their hearts was embroidered in gold *Adieu Jeunesse*. Henry came to them in Russian costume and the evening was spent in feasting, masquing, dancing and music. Late that night the two monarchs rode back, each to his own lodging. In the Val d'Oré their paths crossed and here they said farewell, without ceremony, as they had first greeted each other eighteen days before.

The next day the camps were struck. The pleasure palace was dismantled and shipped back to England. Some of the nobles and many of the servants went home. Others accompanied the King to Calais, where, in a little more than two weeks, Henry was entertaining the Emperor Charles and the noblemen of Spain and the Netherlands. When the French king and his lords knew of this meeting they were full of bitterness. For the moment they could do nothing. War did not break out for another two years. They were too occupied in paying for the splendid, empty show. It was said that many of the French nobility carried their mills, their forests and their farms on their backs. This was true, as they had been forced to mortgage their estates to the silk merchants of Lyons for the wardrobes of costly garments they had worn.

What remained of 'these fierce vanities'? A few descriptions in the dusty pages of the chroniclers; some letters written by sharp-eyed diplomats to their masters in Italy; two pictures painted by order of Henry VIII; and five beautiful bas-reliefs carved in marble in a courtyard at Rouen. Thousands of people carried in their minds glittering memories of the Field of the Cloth of Gold, but one man who had been present, Guillaume Le Roux, the Abbé d'Aumale, brought French and Italian craftsmen to Rouen to carve on the façade of the new wing of his house a representation which time would not efface.

The Progresses of Queen Elizabeth

1558-1603

High above all a cloth of State was spred,
And a rich throne, as bright as sunny day,
On which there sate most brave embellished
With royall robes and gorgeous array,
A mayden Queene, that shone as Titans ray,
In glistring gold, and peerelesse pretious stone:
Yet her bright blazing beautie did assay
To dim the brightnesse of her glorious throne,
As envying herselfe, that too exceeding shone.

EDMUND SPENSER, The Faerie Queene
Booke I, Canto iiii

QUEEN ELIZABETH ON HER WAY TO THE WEDDING OF
ANNE RUSSELL AND LORD HERBERT AT BLACKFRIARS

An Anonymous Painting

Reproduced by courtesy of Colonel F. J. B. Wingfield Digby and the Victoria and Albert Museum

The Progresses of Queen Elizabeth, 1558-1603

WHEN THE UNHAPPY, childless Mary Tudor died on 17 November 1558 at St James's Palace, her sister, Elizabeth, twenty miles away at Hatfield, became not only Queen of England but a free woman. For most of the twenty-five years of her life the new Queen had been surrounded by dangers and distress. She was considered illegitimate. Her mother, Anne Boleyn, had been executed. At the age of fifteen she had found her name involved in a scandal with Thomas Seymour, the Lord Admiral. When her sister, Mary, came to the throne, she was in danger through the strong religious differences between them. She spent two months as a prisoner in the Tower. She was then transferred to semi-captivity at Woodstock and, finally, during the last years of her sister's reign, to a guarded existence at Hatfield. In this retired life she studied under the direction of Roger Ascham. She learned to speak French and Italian as fluently as English; she became an excellent classical scholar; she developed an enduring love of literature and music; and she learned to write an impressive letter in exquisite calligraphy. Her tutor commended not only her aptitude for learning but her love of simplicity. Both these excellent traits may have been her adaptation to the difficulties of her life. Her passion 'to look upon books as soon as the day began to break' remained throughout her life, but her acquiescence in simplicity was only politic. In 1556, Sir Thomas Pope, her guardian, devised a masque for her entertainment, in the great hall at Hatfield, 'where the pageaunts were marvellously furnished'. But the Queen, her sister, disapproved of 'these folliries' and they were held no more. Such were the uneasy conditions of life from which Elizabeth was released by the death of Mary.

After a week spent in preparations the new Queen travelled from Hatfield to the Charterhouse, Lord North's residence, where she remained for five days. She was accompanied by a great train of a thousand noblemen, knights and ladies, and as they rode many must have looked towards her chariot and wondered. What they saw was described about this time by the Venetian ambassador. 'In face she is pleasing rather than beautiful; but her figure is tall and well proportioned. She has a good complexion, though of a somewhat olive tint, beautiful eyes, and above all a beautiful hand, which she likes to show. She is proud and haughty.' This much everyone could see, though some might have added that, like her father, her hair, 'being somewhat red, has the appearance of being gold'. What no one could tell were the thoughts and intentions of this enigmatic lady. Many knew, as did the ambassador, that 'she is of admirable talent and intelligence, of which she has given proof by her behaviour in the dangers and suspicions to which she has been exposed', but she had also learned secrecy by her bitter experience with Seymour and this was to remain a source of lonely strength for the forty-five years of her reign. It plays its part even in the story of her splendour, the apparently superficial account of the rich pageantry of royal pleasures. Did she endear herself to her people on her public appearances by natural good humour? Did she make her great summer progresses, about thirty of them, passing in stately entertainment from one mansion to another, because she loved splendour and sociability? Or were her flashes of unceremonious humour and friendly geniality calculated in effect? And were her visits planned always for subtle reasons of state? Does the truth, perhaps, lie in a tangle of motives like a riddle dropped by this lady when she wearied of it? The answer is far to seek but the questions must be carried in the mind at every moment of this story, from her coronation to her funeral.

On 28 November the Queen went from the Charterhouse to the Tower of London. The first part of the journey was made by chariot but, for the procession through the streets of London, Elizabeth, dressed in purple velvet, rode on horseback, preceded by trumpeters and heralds, the Lord Mayor holding her sceptre, Lord Pembroke bearing her sword. Around her were the sergeants-at-arms and behind her rode Sir Robert Dudley, the Master of the Horse. The people crowded round her; children spoke to her as she passed; there was singing, and musicians played on the little portable organs, called regals. This was more than a royal entry. It was an expression of hope that the days of persecution and gloom had ended. A chronicler noticed 'how comfortable hir presence was to them that went to receive hir on the waie'. She remained some days at the Tower and then made the next stage of her journey by water. Shooting the bridge with trumpets sounding, she was rowed to Somerset House, the great new palace built on the Thames by the Protector. There she remained, while her sister was buried at Westminster Abbey, and on 23 December she rode through streets already being decorated for her coronation, to the palace of Whitehall to keep Christmas.

The preparations for the coronation were swiftly but cautiously made. Dr John Dee, the astrologer, was consulted about the day and he declared, by divination, that Sunday, 15 January, was auspicious. On the previous Thursday the Queen went, again by water, to the Tower of London in readiness for her ceremonial procession through the city to her coronation. She was attended by the Lord Mayor and aldermen in their barge and the barges of the City Guilds, decked with the shields and banners of their mysteries. The barge of the Mercers' Company had 'artillery aboord, shooting off lustilie as they went'. On Saturday morning the Court assembled at the Tower and, although it snowed a little, the great procession set off in the afternoon to make its slow and stately way through the streets to Westminster. It was laid down in the *Liber Regalis*, the Coronation Order used from the time of Edward II, that 'the king on the day before his coronation shall ride bare-headed from the Tower of London through the city to his royal palace at Westminster offering himself to be seen by the people who meet him'. The Queen was carried in an open litter, borne by two mules. She was dressed in a royal robe of cloth of gold and on her red-gold hair was the crown of a princess. She carried no emblems of sovereignty. The Gentlemen Pensioners, chosen from the tallest and handsomest men in England, in gowns of crimson damask, bearing their gilt battle-axes, walked on each side of her. As far as the eye could see there were horsemen, the greatest nobles of the land, all dressed in crimson velvet.

It was a pompous ceremony, not to be hurried even for the cold winds of January. Twelve times she paused at the stages erected in the streets, while children spoke addresses of welcome and elaborate allegorical pageants were performed. On the porch of St Peter's Church stood the waits of the city, 'which did geve a pleasant noyse with their instrumentes as the Quenes majestie did passe by'. From Fenchurch to Cheapside the city companies lined the way, symbols of the wealth and power of the city as they stood in their liveries, wrapped in rich furs, and surrounded by their attendants. Above them, from every window, hung banners and decorations of cloth of gold. In Cheapside the Lord Mayor and the aldermen waited to receive her. The Recorder presented her with a purse of crimson satin, richly wrought with gold, containing a thousand gold marks. The Queen replied to his oration with a speech so direct and pithy that all who listened marvelled that it could be phrased by so young a princess. Thence she passed to Temple Bar, where she found the two giants, Gotmagot and Corineus, holding Latin verses in their hands, and 'a noyse of singing children', one of whom, beautifully dressed as a poet, said farewell to the Queen on behalf of the city in four rhymed stanzas. Elizabeth replied, 'Be ye well assured I will

stande your good Quene'. Waving her hands and showing a merry face to all the crowd, the Queen went through Temple Bar to Westminster, leaving memories of many pleasant words spoken to children and old people; of the spray of rosemary given to her by a poor woman at Fleet Bridge, which she carried with her for the rest of the journey; of the firm, strong, simple words of her speeches; of her desire to win the hearts of the people, which she expressed 'in coupling mildness with majesty, in stately stooping to the meanest sort'.

The following day Elizabeth was crowned in Westminster Abbey by Oglethorpe, Bishop of Carlisle. The see of Canterbury was vacant owing to the death of Cardinal Pole; the Archbishop of York and most of the bishops refused to officiate because they were opposed to her religious views. The Queen was superbly arrayed in cloth of gold, and silver tissue, furred with powdered ermines. She protested at the anointing that 'the oil was grease, and smelled ill', but otherwise the service followed its accustomed ceremonies. She was girt with the sword, symbolizing strength, had the bracelets, signifying good works, placed on her arms, and received the two crowns. Then, in full regalia but with an easy informality of manner, she passed to Westminster Hall for the banquet. Here, as at the other events of these first days of her reign, she won instant popularity. A sober Italian spectator thought that, in doing so, 'she exceeded the bounds of gravity and decorum', but her own people were swift to approve that she was not like those whose behaviour, in Bacon's words, 'is like a verse, wherein every Syllable is measured'. This popularity must be maintained. She succeeded in maintaining it by a device which suited her personal inclinations, the desires of her people and the obscurer purposes of diplomacy.

Elizabeth inherited from her father and absorbed from the atmosphere of her time a sensuous delight in pageantry. Henry VIII led the vogue for disguisings, and his court became the centre of those acts which made a swift and brilliant appeal to the eye and ear. If Elizabeth had gratified this delight by following her father's tradition she would have staged court masques at great expense for the pleasure of a few favourites, but this would have conflicted with her frugal nature and hampered the spread of her popularity. She decided to make her summer holidays the occasions of royal pageantry on a national scale, and these progresses, which commenced with a visit to Essex in 1561 and continued until 1601, only a little more than a year before her death, were arranged to carry her, with ceremony, entertainment and rejoicing, through two or three counties. She stayed at the houses of the nobility. The honour of being the Queen's host was eagerly sought and, when granted, was a sign of the highest favour. It was a costly distinction, because, although the food and often the

The Quenes maiestie In her litter
vnder the canapie borne by

The lord Robert Dudley m̃r
of the Horfes
leading the
paffrey of honor

The lorde ambrofe
dudley leading the
fecond litter horfe

The lorde giles paulet
leading the firste
litter horfe

Above: QUEEN ELIZABETH PROCEEDING TO
PARLIAMENT

An Original Drawing in a Manuscript begun by Thomas Hawley,
College of Arms

College of Arms

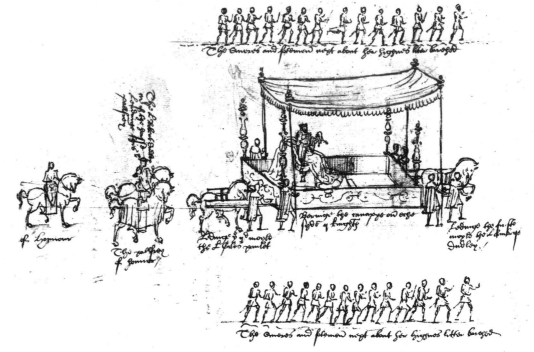

Right: QUEEN ELIZABETH'S PROCESSION TO HER
CORONATION

An Original Drawing by an Anonymous Herald

British Museum

furnishings were provided by the Royal Household, every host felt a desire to surpass his neighbours in rich gifts and lavish entertainment. It was an axiom that the displays 'should be graced with elegancy', not 'daubed with Cost' but sometimes taste and wealth went hand-in-hand, as for instance when the gentlemen of Suffolk rode to the county boundary to receive Her Majesty, two hundred young gentlemen clad all in white velvet, three hundred of the graver sort in black velvet with gold chains, attended by fifteen hundred serving men.

The most splendid of these royal visits was the progress to the Midlands in 1575, when nearly three weeks were spent in spectacular revels at Kenilworth Castle. The handsome and courtly Earl of Leicester had often been high in the royal favour and had even been spoken of as a suitor for the Queen's hand. Perhaps he wearied of waiting upon her indecision, for not long before the visit he secretly married the dowager Lady Sheffield. It was imperative that the Queen should not know this. The princely pleasures of Kenilworth, an event of Italianate magnificence devised for a queen who understood pageantry, had a background as complicated as a game of chess. It was said that Elizabeth undertook these visits, not only to seal her popularity with the masses, but to undermine the power and impoverish the resources of her great nobles. If such were her intentions when she went to Kenilworth, what were the purposes of her astute host in inviting her?

The Earl of Leicester met the Queen at Long Ichington, seven miles from Kenilworth but still within his territory. There, in a magnificent pavilion, he entertained her at dinner, after which they rode to the castle, hunting as they went. They came to Kenilworth at eight o'clock on a summer evening. As they rode through the park ten sybils, clad in white silk, greeted the Queen. Then a huge porter rushed from the gate, complaining of the disturbance. When his eye lighted upon the Queen, he dropped his club and yielded up the keys of the castle. Then, as Elizabeth moved forward, six giants, eight feet high, appeared on the ramparts and sounded a fanfare of welcome on silver trumpets five feet long. They played as she passed into the first courtyard, where on the lake before the castle was a floating island, blazing with torches. On it sat the Lady of the Lake, arrayed in rich silks and attended by damsels. As her island approached the shore, she addressed a speech of submission to the Queen. From this courtyard was erected a stately bridge over the moat, so that the Queen could pass into the castle between pillars bearing gifts from the gods. The significance of these was explained as they rode by a poet dressed in sky-blue and crimson silk. When the Queen had been conveyed to her chamber darkness had fallen. There was a salvo of guns and then the night sky was lit by the delicate tracery of fireworks. This was a

special pleasure to the Queen, who had seen a firework display for the first time only three years before. Her host gratified her delight to the full and then added a surprise. The flashing lights had been reflected in the waters of the lake and as a climax rockets were lit which skimmed the surface of the water in an erratic course, taking dives beneath the surface, after which 'they would rise and mount out of the water again'.

Diversions to fill every hour of the Queen's days followed one another with princely splendour. There were hunting and bear-baiting by day, dancing, music, fireworks and various entertainments at night. One evening a savage rushed out of the wood by torchlight to make his obeisance to the Queen. In his enthusiasm he over-stepped his part and flung a branch of a tree near Elizabeth's horse. The animal reared with fright, the attendants rushed forward, but the Queen cried, 'No hurt! No hurt!' and won more hearts. A barge, filled with 'very delectable muzik', came across the water in the sunset. An Italian acrobat tumbled with marvellous ease and agility. There were morris dancers. The Coventry men performed their ancient play of *Hock Tuesday*, which the Queen liked so well that she gave them money and commanded them to play it before her again. A mermaid eighteen feet long greeted the Queen from the lake. A consort of six instruments, riding in a dolphin, played their music on the water. The hours of the night were shortened by banquets and masques. The Queen ate little but delighted in the entertainments, all except Master Gascoigne's *Zabeta*, the performance of which was cancelled. Was it that there was no time, the weather was not seasonable, or that the verses pressed on the Queen too insistently the advantages of marriage?

On 27 July the Queen walked for the last time through the acre of specially constructed herb garden; she looked again at the hundreds of rare birds fluttering in their vast cage, painted in imitation of jewels; she said farewell to her host and continued her progress to Charterley, to Stafford, to Worcester and finally to Woodstock. This palace held mixed memories for Elizabeth. Here she had lived a semi-prisoner, surrounded by the guards set by her sister. Now her visit was of another kind. Around her was her own court and from near and far came flocking the simple, ordinary people, whose affection she had won. Even those who came near offending her, as Gascoigne had at Kenilworth, could be forgiven if they pleased her. Gascoigne now pronounced before Her Majesty *The Tale of Hemetes the Heremyte* and then presented her with the text translated into French, Latin and Italian. It was a dignified occasion, with displays of learning and loyalty in Latin orations, but the easy summer air had gone. It was September and the Queen hastened back to London and the complicated intrigues of her court.

A YEOMAN OF THE GUARD ATTENDING
QUEEN ELIZABETH ON A PROGRESS
From Nichols's 'Progresses of Queen Elizabeth'
British Museum

QUEEN ELIZABETH'S SEAL
British Museum

GEORGE GASCOIGNE PRESENTING HIS BOOK,
'THE TALE OF HEMETES THE HERMYTE
PRONOWNCED BEFORE THE Q. MAJESTY AT
WOODSTOCKE, 1575'

British Museum

As the years passed these intrigues became maze-like in their convolutions, but in 1588 a mortal danger arose which gloriously straightened the path of the Queen and her people. Philip of Spain had been threatening war for years. Elizabeth fenced with him but, as the chief Protestant monarch, could not avoid giving him causes of offence. It was known that the *Armada* was preparing in the Spanish ports. Drake delayed its mobilization by his daring raid on Cadiz, but in the summer of 1588 Philip, after days spent in prayer, decided to make a devastating attack upon England. On 19 July news arrived that the *Armada* was off the Lizard. Drake sailed from Plymouth to meet the Spanish ships and commenced a running fight up the Channel. The fear in every English heart was that the *Armada* would make contact with the Prince of Parma in the Netherlands, thus allowing the strong Spanish armies to pour across the narrow sea. Troops for the defence of London were sent to Tilbury. 'It was a pleasant sight to beholde the souldiers as they marched towards Tylbury, their cheerefull countenances, couragious wordes and gestures, dauncing and leaping wheresoever they came.' In the last days of the month the *Armada* was dislodged from Calais with fireships and its remnants were driven in helpless confusion to try to make the perilous journey home round the north of Scotland. News travelled slowly; the danger of invasion still seemed imminent; so the Queen decided to visit her troops. To the sound of trumpets and drums she swept down the river in the royal barge. Landing, she mounted her white horse and, holding a general's truncheon in her hand, she rode alone through the ranks of the army. When all were arrayed before her, she addressed them in the most inspired of her speeches. Over the gap of nearly four hundred years the resonant voice rolls from the Essex marshes. 'I know I have but the body of a weak and feeble woman, but I have the heart and stomach of a king, and of a king of England too; and think foul scorn that Parma or Spain, or any prince of Europe, should dare to invade the borders of my realm.' The response was eager and tremendous. The men waited impatiently for the arrival of Parma and heard the news of the defeat of the *Armada* with open disappointment. Four months later the Queen passed through the streets of London in a throne-like chariot, drawn by two white horses, to make public thanksgiving at St Paul's Cathedral for the deliverance of her country.

Elizabeth was no longer young. The cares of a long reign were many and heavy, but she was strong and vigorous. When the danger of invasion had passed she began her progresses again, bidding the old stay behind and the young and able go with her. Her suitor and most lavish host, the Earl of Leicester, had died a few weeks after he, as commander of the army, had welcomed her at Tilbury. But there was a new suitor of a different sort. The Earl of Hertford had incurred the Queen's displeasure by a marriage which seemed dangerous to her throne. He and his wife suffered grievous punishment and after his release from prison he needed to win the favour of the Queen. So he invited her to his house at Elvetham for a three days' visit in 1591. In his lavish hospitality there were echoes of that other great reception at Kenilworth—the lake with three islands, the poet dressed in green silk, the virgins who strewed flowers before the Queen and sang a sweet song of six parts, the fireworks, the orations, and the splendid banquets. There were the same princely pleasures, but with a difference. As the Queen drove away through the park, past the oak tree which she planted and which still stands, the musicians sang 'O come again, sweet beauties sunne: When thou art gone, our joyes are done'. The Queen was nearly sixty. Would she come again? She suffered recurrent fits of melancholy but she still enjoyed the gaiety of life. In 1600 she attended the wedding of Anne Russell and Henry, Lord Herbert, at Blackfriars. She was the guest of Lord Cobham and was carried from the riverside to Lady Russell's house in a litter borne by six noblemen. That night there was a memorable masque of eight ladies in cloth of silver and carnation taffeta, with their hair loose about their shoulders. One of them begged the Queen to dance. Her majesty asked what she was. 'Affection', replied the lady. 'Affection', said the Queen, 'is false'. But she rose and danced.

So the glory of her long reign came slowly to an end in brooding and obstinate silence. At Christmas 1602, Dr Dee, her faithful occult adviser, warned her not to remain at Whitehall, so the court moved to her favourite palace at Richmond. Even this was of no avail. The Queen's health failed visibly. She could not be persuaded to touch any physic, or to eat, or to go to bed. At last her old friend, the Lord Admiral, was brought to her and, half-persuaded, half-carried, she was put to bed. She refused all remedies. One of the watchers said, 'She grew worse because she would be so.' Archbishop Whitgift, her 'black husband' as she called him, prayed by the bedside, and as he prayed, the Queen fell into a deep sleep from which she never woke.

Queen Elizabeth died of a settled melancholy, but when she was buried a month later it was fitting that the pageant should be rich and noble, as a symbol of the splendour of her reign. The coffin, surmounted by a crowned effigy, was drawn by four sombrely caparisoned horses. She had no family to mourn her and around her bier were her Gentlemen Pensioners, the tallest and handsomest men in England, who had seen all her great triumphs, walking bare-headed with their halberds downwards.

QUEEN ELIZABETH'S ENTERTAINMENT BY THE EARL OF HERTFORD AT ELVETHAM, 1591

In the possession of the author

Aigle Vuianve comme aussi le reue des animaulx coureurs.

II. Musique

Le Dieu Apollon auec ses 9. Muses

Diane auec ses trois Charies

A SECTION FROM A VELLUM ROLL OF THE PROCESSIONS AND TOURNAMENT AT HEIDELBERG

Victoria and Albert Museum

The Wedding of Princess Elizabeth and Count Frederick

1613

So when my Mistress shall be seen
  In sweetness of her looks and mind,
By virtue first, then choice, a Queen,
  Tell me, if she were not design'd
The eclipse and glory of her kind?

SIR HENRY WOTTON, To Elizabeth of Bohemia

The Wedding of Princess Elizabeth and Count Frederick, 1613

IT WAS ST VALENTINE'S DAY in the year 1613. February, the month when, as the proverb says, the sun is dearly won; the fourteenth, the central day of the year's bleakest weather. But that year the February climate was not bleak; it was warm and wet. St Valentine's Day occurred in an interval between the showers, and the sun was shining as a procession wound its way through the intricate maze of galleries and courtyards of Whitehall Palace, from the presence-chamber to the stairs of the great chamber and thence to the Chapel Royal. All the way there was a throng of happy people, crowding to watch and making room as the first noblemen appeared with a burst of trumpets. The procession was in four parts, 'in all the Pomp and Glory that so much Grandure could express', but it was to see one person that all those merry people had crowded along the lanes from Charing Cross and Westminster. First came the procession of Frederick, Count Palatine of the Rhine, led by the Duke of Lennox and the Earl of Nottingham, the Lord High Admiral. Around him were the peers of the German states and the unmarried peers of England and Scotland. He was a handsome youth, his dark complexion and self-confident bearing set off by a silver suit, embroidered with gold and diamonds. This was the boy who had come to marry England's beautiful princess, Elizabeth, the daughter of James I. The crowds liked what they saw of him, but it was Elizabeth they wished to see. Escorted by her brother, Charles, and the Earl of Northampton, she passed gaily through the spectators. She wore a gown of Florence cloth of silver, richly embroidered. Upon her head was a crown of gold from which hung pendants of diamonds and pearls to mingle with her long, fair hair. Her train was supported by sixteen young ladies, one for each year of her age, dressed in jewelled white satin. As they went into the gloom of the great staircase with the trumpets echoing, it seemed to the onlookers that her passage was like a milky way. The two processions of the King and Queen attracted little notice, although the rather ungainly James, in his sumptuous suit of black velvet, with a diamond of wonderful lustre in his hat, mourning for his son, the Prince of Wales, stirred feelings of awe and sympathy. Owing to the confined space of the Chapel only a few of the highest nobles were able to enter. The others clustered round outside, listening to the sweet strains of the music specially composed by Dr John Bull for his young mistress and pupil.

Elizabeth was born at Falkland Castle in August 1596. Her father had not yet succeeded to the throne of England, and was ruling Scotland as James VI. She did not live with her parents, as her father believed that children should be brought up by strangers. His theory was strengthened by the discovery that the Scots suspected his wife, Anne of Denmark, of Catholic tendencies and continually rebuked her on account of her 'vanity', 'night waking and balling'. The little princess was entrusted first to the care of the Earl of Linlithgow, and after 1603 to that of Lord and Lady Harrington at Combe Abbey in Warwickshire. Her father and mother found themselves transferred from poverty to opulence. Their extravagances became boundless, his in the direction of displays of wealth to bolster a pathetic show of power, hers in the rich profusion which the arts could bring to luxurious living. The royal children, separated from one another and from their parents, were brought up with the most delicate regard for their future positions as rich, powerful, and cultivated princes. From an early age Elizabeth was proficient in French, a knowledge which was to serve a romantic purpose, for when Frederick came to woo her it was their only common tongue. The influence of her father, whose love of learning was almost pedantic, was seen in her ability to write a beautifully-phrased letter, and throughout her childhood she wrote him reports of her progress. But the taste of her mother directed her love of poetry and music, her exquisite calligraphy and her passion for superfluously lovely things. She owned a Venetian virginal, brilliantly decorated with pictures in coloured glass, plaques of silver foliage, and representations of birds in exquisite coloured enamels. As she came to adolescence her affection for her elder brother, Henry, strengthened by separation, occupied a central place in her heart, and she expressed it in some of the most beautiful letters ever written by sister to brother. Her regard for him, showing through the well-chosen words and informing the neatly designed handwriting, was finally revealed in the directions written in gold ink and in the gaily coloured strands of floss silk twisted with tinsel thread with which she secured the letters.

From the age of fourteen she lived at Kew, still in the care of the Harringtons. At once she moved into the circle of the court. She had rooms in the Cockpit at Whitehall where she stayed when she visited her parents, travelling on the Thames in her own barge. The Queen, preoccupied with the elegant distractions of festivities, so that the court became 'a continued maskarado, where she and her ladies, like so many nymphs or Nereides, made the night more glorious than the day', brought out her daughter and her younger son, Charles, in *Tethys Festival* by Samuel Daniel. These lovely children, in Inigo Jones's robes 'of greene satin imbrodered with golden flowers', appeared 'to the ravishment of the beholders'. Elizabeth was happy in the midst of all this splendour, seeing much of her two brothers, riding with them, hunting with them, acting with them—and when she was happy she was gay. Poets celebrated her beauty and her vivacity. Her fame spread far from the borders of her country, and great princes in need of a consort sent discreet messages to London. The Dauphin, Maurice, Prince of Orange, Gustavus Adolphus, Philip III of Spain—they all thought of the beautiful English princess, with her long golden tresses and her infectious laughter. Some were rejected by her father, for reasons of state; others did not please Elizabeth, on more personal grounds. There were rumours of an eligible young man at Heidelberg, not only a Protestant but handsome, and only four days older than herself. Her mother favoured the match with Philip, who shared her extravagant love of courtly splendour, and she tried to tease her away from the new suitor by nick-naming her 'Goody Palsgrave'. But Elizabeth, perhaps remembering that Philip was over thirty, retorted 'I would rather espouse a Protestant Count than a Catholic Emperor'.

At Heidelberg feverish preparations were made for the departure of the young Count Palatine. His steward, Count Meinhard von Schonberg, had visited England in July 1612 and had reported on his return that, personable as the boy was, he might not appear dignified enough in the sophisticated English court. The magnificent Duke of Wurtenburg's dancing master was borrowed for a month to teach him deportment and dancing. The goldsmiths of Heidelberg were employed making sumptuous gifts for him to take, and liveries of unusual splendour were provided for the one hundred and fifty attendants who were to escort him. The Palatine States were not unaccustomed to splendour. The Count's father, the Elector Frederick IV, had delighted to surround himself with pomp, but, at his death in 1610, the court passed under the influence of his widow, a daughter of William the Silent, Prince of Orange. She determined that her son, who, at the age of eighteen, would succeed his father as Elector and head of the Protestant States of Europe, should be trained for those positions, and should make a marriage that would assist him to maintain them. When his education was complete, his steward was sent to London to negotiate for the hand of Elizabeth, daughter of the richest Protestant king in Europe. The mission was successful, and in the autumn of 1612 Frederick set out for England.

His crossing was not without incident. First he was delayed by contrary winds; then, having sailed, his ships were damaged, and he put back to port. Three ships of the English fleet were sent to conduct him and, on 16 October, after a bad passage, he landed at Gravesend. Immediately the formality of the court surrounded him. He was welcomed by the Master of the Ceremonies, and arrangements were made for him to stay at Gravesend until his clothes arrived in his own ships. The Master of the Wardrobe came to greet him on behalf of the King, and he was importuned by the Steward of the Royal Household, the Duke of Lennox, to continue his journey to London without delay. He was not to worry about the absence of his fine suits as the King would receive him *en famille*. Twenty-four royal barges were waiting and he was rowed up the Thames in the afternoon of 18 October. From the Tower to White-hall great crowds stood in the cold rain of an autumn dusk to see him pass. It was almost dark when the Count, standing by the open windows of the barge to show himself to the people, dimly saw the straggling mass of red brick buildings of White-hall Palace and a cluster of lights at the Privy Stairs. As he landed, Prince Charles, a boy of twelve but already a courtier, stepped forward to greet him and led him to the new banqueting-room, blazing with torches. The King advanced three steps from his chair of state and embraced him. Frederick bore himself well but he was nervous, especially as the Queen was obviously distant. His French compliments were spoken in so low a voice that no one heard them. The sight of Elizabeth, standing beside her parents, seemed to banish his fears. With a swift action he stooped to kiss the hem of her gown, but, with a movement as easy as his own, she made a great curtsy and stopped him with her hand. As they rose he kissed her.

Essex House, in the Strand, was lent to him as his residence, but he also had rooms at Whitehall and in Prince Henry's palace of St James's. The round of pleasures needed only the excitement of a wedding in the air to send it spinning on its way. There was a City pageant and a banquet at Guildhall, supper parties at the palaces and a play given by the Princess's own company at the Cockpit. One shadow on all this happiness was the sudden illness of Prince Henry. The King and Queen, Elizabeth and Frederick went to see him, but within a few days it was known that the case was hopeless, and the King, who hated illness, left at once for the country. In spite of orders that no one should visit the invalid except his doctors, the clergy and his attendants, his devoted sister made many attempts to reach his bedside, even once disguising herself as a page. On 6 November, Henry, a prince on whose boyish achievements the people had built a pyramid of expectation, died of typhoid fever.

FREDERICK, THE ELECTOR PALATINE
Miniature attributed to Peter Oliver

Reproduced by courtesy of His Grace the Duke of Buccleuch

ENGRAVING SYMBOLIZING
THE MARRIAGE OF
PRINCESS ELIZABETH AND
THE ELECTOR PALATINE

British Museum

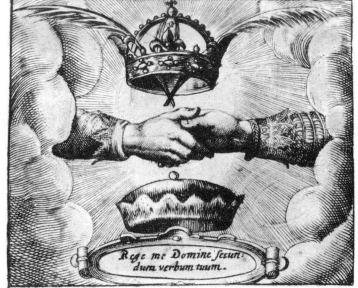

Rege me Domine secundum verbum tuum.

ELIZABETH OF BOHEMIA
Miniature by Isaac Oliver, Windsor Castle

Reproduced by gracious permission of His Majesty the King

[25]

British Museum

THE PROCESSION OF PRINCESS ELIZABETH AND FREDERICK TO THE CHAPEL ROYAL, 14 February 1613

It was a difficult time for the young Count. His princess was heart-broken at the death of her brother; the King was apt to behave oddly under conditions of stress. But Frederick offered his condolences in appropriate passages from the Bible, and James roused himself, saying, 'he would have nothing in his Eye, to bring so sad a Message to his Heart', and plunged into 'the jollity, feasting and magnificence of Christmas'. This commenced with a private investiture of Frederick as a Knight of the Order of the Garter. The jewel of St George on the collar was a gift to him from Elizabeth. Two days after Christmas the private ceremony of betrothal took place in the Banqueting House. The Princess wore a superb gown of black satin brocaded with silver flowers, and she set a fashion by wearing a plume of white feathers in her hair. The Count remembered the young prince by appearing in a suit of purple velvet. The old gaiety was spontaneously bubbling up. When the Chief Secretary translated the formal sentences into rather inelegant French, Elizabeth burst into laughter. The Queen did not attend any of these events.

During the next six weeks the handsome couple were often seen riding in the parks. They saw fourteen plays, of which six were by Shakespeare. They spent long hours in each other's company, but Elizabeth did not neglect her father. Every evening she went to Whitehall to play cards or billiards with him. At the New Year there was a lavish exchange of gifts, which was made even more sumptuous by the long-awaited announcement of the date of the wedding. Frederick was anxious to return to his own country, but the King, unwilling to lose his daughter so soon after the death of his son, had been reluctant to fix a date. The splendid jewels from Heidelberg were the cause of much admiration. Frederick gave Elizabeth a set of diamond ornaments, the ear-rings having the finest pearls in Christendom. To both the King and Queen he gave a bottle and a large cup, each carved from a single agate. In the few weeks to St Valentine's Day there were many preparations to make. The Princess took up her residence at St James's Palace and personally supervised the preparation of her trousseau—silk stockings, underwear of cobweb lawn, fine Holland cloth for curtains and sheets, blankets from Milan, down pillows sewn with silk, quilts cased in taffetas and the great bridal bedstead, the four corners of the canopy surmounted by eight plumes of feathers decorated with Venice gold and spangles. Frederick left her to this congenial occupation and went hunting with Prince Charles. He returned for his public installation as a Knight of the Garter at Windsor and then joined Elizabeth for the opening of the public rejoicings on 11 February. This took the form of a mock battle on the Thames, with an unprecedented display of fireworks. By the time the vanquished Turkish admiral was conveyed to the palace stairs only Elizabeth and Frederick were there in the chill dusk to receive his submission. The King was tired of all the shooting and had withdrawn to his apartments.

The crowd outside the Chapel Royal stirred during the long service. They knew that the royal family, the Count, and his uncle, Prince Henry of Nassau, were on a dais in the middle of the chapel. They had seen the gold and silver tapestries, based on designs by Raphael, which covered the walls. It pleased them that the service was according to the Book of Common Prayer in English and especially that Frederick had learned his part. They heard the music of Bull's setting of the Benediction, and knew that, in the pause that followed, the health of the bride and bridegroom was being drunk in a great golden bowl. Then those who were nearest the door caught a whisper which was eagerly passed round. During the ceremony 'some Lightnings and Coruscations of Joy appear'd in her Countenance that express'd more than an ordinary smile, being almost elated to a Laughter'. As this little tale was passed deeper into the crowd, the guards made a way and Elizabeth came slowly from the chapel. The smile was still upon her lips and now seemed to radiate throughout her whole being. There was a dashing air about Frederick as he strode along, preceded by six young German gallants, clad in crimson velvet and gold lace, bearing silver trumpets. When he entered the banqueting house they greeted him with a merry flourish.

The rest of this day and the succeeding days were lost in a stream of costly pleasure. The banquet was served in a dining-room specially built on the terrace in the Sermon Court. Full of delight, Elizabeth changed into a gown of cloth of gold and went with her husband and the royal party to see Campion's *The Lords Maske* performed by twelve peers in the Banqueting House. It was sumptuously staged with Inigo Jones's striking effect of 'eight Starres of extraordinarie bignesse, fixed between the Firmament and the Earth'. But it was over-long for a wedding night, and there were signs of pleasure when the stars were transformed into masquers, with whom the young couple danced before they said good night. The next day the King paid an early visit with costly gifts of jewels; there was tilting in the afternoon, and at night a masque by George Chapman offered by the Middle Temple and Lincoln's Inn. This was the most popular of the wedding entertainments, especially a dance of twelve little boys dressed like baboons. The actors adhered to tradition by arriving on horseback and in open chariots, accompanied by Indian torch-bearers. This feature was so successful that the men of Gray's Inn and the Inner Temple decided to make their arrival for the third night's entertainment by a torchlit procession on the river. It attracted so many people that the actors could not get into the hall, and the performance was postponed until the Saturday. Elizabeth's own company was preparing a play for that day, so the royal guests saw *The Dutch Courtesan* in the afternoon and the masque at night.

There seemed no end to the pleasures scattered before the lovely princess and her husband, but the King was already thinking of the cost. He dismissed many of the members of the household he had engaged for Frederick and begged him to curb the prodigality of his gifts. The climax of the Count's generosity was the gift of a pair of magnificent French chariots for Elizabeth and her mother. This present, together with the young man's amiable manner, did much to win over the Queen from her former disapproval. But Frederick had no wish to linger in the expensive luxury of the English court. He sent some of his attendants back to Germany and urged the reluctant king to fix the date of Elizabeth's departure. After many hesitations James agreed to allow her to leave after Easter. Preparations were swiftly made. Four Royal Commissioners were appointed to escort her; attendants and servants were engaged; the Lord High Admiral was ordered, as his last official act, to provide seven warships and many merchantmen, with two thousand five hundred mariners, to convey the Princess across the water. All was ready by Easter, and on the following Saturday the royal party left Whitehall in a fleet of state barges and went down the river to Greenwich. A few days were spent quietly there, while many people, sincerely moved by the departure of the Princess, came to kiss her hand in farewell. They rode on to Rochester, where the parting with her parents took place. It was a sad occasion, but the sharp pain of separation was eased by the fact that her dear brother, Charles, was to stay with her until she embarked. She watched her parents drive away. Then the princely cavalcade moved to Canterbury. Elizabeth lodged at the Deanery, waiting for news of a favourable wind. For six days she waited, enjoying in a constrained way her last sight of England and the pleasure of her brother's companionship. Then the King sent word to Charles, ordering him to return to London. The final break was at hand. These two children consoled themselves by planning how they would visit each other at Heidelberg and London. The Prince rode back to London, and Elizabeth went to her ship at Margate, their hearts full of future meetings, which never came to pass.

The ship in which she was to sail was the *Prince Royal*, the great vessel built only three years before by Phineas Pett in honour of her elder brother. She was received on board by the Lord High Admiral. Orders were given for the fleet to form into a crescent, and all was ready for departure. But the wind turned easterly, and the royal passengers were disembarked, to spend three nights uncomfortably in the little village of Margate. On the evening of 25 April they went on board again and the next morning they sailed, under the care of a skilful Dutch pilot sent by Prince Maurice of Nassau. The following night they saw the lights of Ostend.

The Princess was received in the United Provinces with every mark of respect and affection. Her natural gaiety broke forth again as she went on the canals from town to town. After fourteen days as the guest of Prince Maurice, she came to Arnhem and passed by stages to Bonn. Her husband had gone on to Heidelberg to prepare her welcome but she had many noble escorts and a following of four thousand persons. At Bonn the Prince of Brandenberg handed her on to a beautiful vessel specially built by Frederick's orders for the passage of the Rhine. The private cabins were hung with rose and blue velvet. There was another fine vessel for the Commissioners and thirty Rhine boats for her attendants. In stately procession this water pageant moved up the Rhine. Elizabeth was eager to see her own territory and as the boats came near to Bacharach she knew that she was at home. A fast chaloupe darted down the river and her husband leaped on board her vessel. They travelled together to Frankenthal, one of Elizabeth's dower towns, where the inhabitants prepared a magnificent reception. On 7 June, in doubtful weather, the Princess drove towards Heidelberg in the chariot Frederick had given her in London. She wore a robe of cloth of gold and a riding hat of crimson velvet plumed with feathers. A considerable way outside the city the Count met her. He transferred her to his state coach, the handsomest in Europe. Preceded by a troop of cavalry in scarlet, green and white uniforms and with her husband on horseback by her side, she drove into Heidelberg between five thousand troops drawn up in battle array. She passed beneath a triumphal arch sixty-five feet high, up to the castle on the hill, where her mother-in-law, the lady who had planned this match, was waiting to receive her.

For a month the city kept holiday, and the court spread its pleasures before her. But gradually the momentum slackened; the English visitors took their departure, and the Princess Elizabeth was left alone in her new home. There were sad moments when her dear friends, Lord and Lady Harrington, with whom she had lived for nearly ten years, came to say farewell. They encouraged her with thoughts of her great station and of all that the future held for her as consort of the leader of the Protestant princes of Europe. The thoughts cheered her, because she did not know that her husband would lose the Palatinate in seven years; that she would be Queen of Bohemia for so short a time that she would be called *The Winter Queen* in derision; that she would never see her parents and her brother again; that she would not return to England for nearly fifty years, and then only to die. But she also did not know that others would call her, with feelings far from derision, *The Queen of Hearts*, and that she would be the link between two royal dynasties when her grandson, the Elector of Hanover, became George I, King of England.

FREDERICK GREETING ELIZABETH OUTSIDE HEIDELBERG
An Engraving by Keller, from 'Beschreibung der Reiss . . . Heyraths' 1613

British Museum

A TORCH-BEARER IN THE
'MEMORABLE MASKE'
BY GEORGE CHAPMAN
15 February, 1613 (Walpole Society, No. 60)
Chatsworth Estates Company

A MASKER IN 'THE LORD'S MASKE' BY THOMAS CAMPION
14 February, 1613 (Walpole Society, No. 58)
Chatsworth Estates Company

A PAGE, LIKE A FIERY SPIRIT,
IN 'THE LORD'S MASKE'
BY THOMAS CAMPION
14 February, 1613 (Walpole Society, No. 59)
Chatsworth Estates Company

THE MASKERS
Original Drawings by Inigo Jones

THE ELECTOR PALATINE LEAVING ENGLAND WITH HIS BRIDE
A Painting by Adam Willaerts

Trustees of the National Maritime Museum

[31]

THE DUKE OF WURTEMBURG
A Section from a Vellum Roll of the Processions and Tournament at Heidelberg
Victoria and Albert Museum

THE RESTORATION OF CHARLES II
A Painting attributed to I. Fuller
Reproduced by courtesy of Vivian E. Cornelius, Esq.

The Restoration, Coronation and Wedding of Charles II

1660-1-2

1660, 3rd May. Came the most happy tidings of his Majesty's gracious declaration and applications to the Parliament, General, and People, and their dutiful acceptance and acknowledgment, after a most bloody and unreasonable rebellion of near twenty years. Praised be for ever the Lord of Heaven, who only doeth wondrous things, because His mercy endureth for ever.

JOHN EVELYN, Diary

The Restoration, Coronation and Wedding of Charles II, 1660-1-2

ON 4 APRIL 1660 a troop of dusty horsemen rode through the streets of Breda, their arrival causing excited comment amongst the townspeople. In the centre was a young man 'with a swarthy complexion agreeing well with his fine black eyes, a large ugly mouth', who, as he dismounted, it was easy to see was very tall and well-made, with 'a graceful and dignified carriage and a fine figure'. Charles Stuart had come to set up his court in this strongly-fortified town just across the water from his own country. He was a king in name only, his stark Presbyterian coronation at Scone in 1651 having brought him nothing but defeat and misery. Now the situation had changed. Cromwell was dead, the Puritan factions wrangled over the succession, and everywhere people whispered of the King's coming. Every day messengers slipped out of London and made their way across to Flushing; Pepys wrote that 'every man begins to be merry and full of hopes', and the Protestant princes of Europe gathered at Breda to give their support to Charles in the turn of his fortune. With the advice of Sir John Grenville, who had been faithful to him through all his troubles, Charles drafted a letter to the two Houses of Parliament, the Army, the Navy and the City of London, declaring his democratic intentions. This was carried with all speed to London, but was locked up for some days by Parliament while they kept a fast. On 1 May the letter was read to both Houses, the members standing bare-headed, and an answer was returned thanking His Majesty for his gracious letter. 'In all this,' said Pepys 'there was not so much as one No.' Jubilation broke forth—bonfires, bells, toasts to the King drunk by people upon their knees in the streets, which, thought Pepys, 'is a little too much'. But nothing seemed too much to the exiles in Holland, who, with the promise of a grant of £50,000 from Parliament and gifts of £1,000 from each of the twelve city Companies, were preparing for their joyful return to England.

Charles decided to go by water to The Hague, calling at Delft on the way. A flotilla of thirteen state yachts was provided for his journey, with floating kitchens attached, in which were to be prepared banquets of twenty-five courses. This was the first time that the English exiles had seen these swift sailing boats, and when the King expressed his pleasure in them the magistrates of Amsterdam gave him, for his use on the Thames, a superb vessel made for the Dutch East India Company, decorated with paintings by the best Dutch masters. The royal flotilla sailed before a strong wind for Dordrecht, where Sir John Grenville, that moment arrived from England, came on board with the stirring news that events had moved so rapidly that the English fleet, commanded by Sir Edward Montagu, was now lying off Scheveningen, waiting to carry the King back to his native land. Immediately the plans were altered. The King decided to sail on during the night, to arrive at Delft at daybreak, and there to change immediately into state carriages for the final stage of the journey to The Hague. All the preparations for a state entry were thrown into disorder by this precipitate arrival, but people from all the neighbouring towns, eager to see this handsome king who, by what seemed a miracle, was about to recover the throne of his ancestors, crowded the streets of the beautiful little city.

Charles drove straight to the palace of Prince Maurice of Nassau, which had been furnished for his reception. Waiting to greet him at the head of the stairs, was his aunt, Elizabeth, Queen of Bohemia. Their meeting was affectionate, but the King's haste had exhausted himself as well as his companions. He expressed a wish to dine alone, and everyone went early to bed. The rest was needed, as bad weather prevented the fleet sailing for a week and the time was spent in receptions, banquets, touching for the king's evil, dancing and accepting gifts. The most magnificent of these was a bedstead of crimson velvet embroidered with silver, presented to him by the States of Holland. It had been made in Paris at a cost of £8,000 for the Prince of Orange, but, owing to his untimely death, it had never been used. At last the weather improved and the farewell receptions were held. On 23 May the King rode on to the sands at Scheveningen, entered the admiral's barge hung with tapestries, and was rowed to the flag ship, the *Nazeby*. Pepys, who was on board as the admiral's secretary recorded that there was 'infinite shooting off of the guns'. He saw the royal family dine alone in the coach next to the great cabin, and then the sad parting of the King from his aunt and his sister. The ladies were rowed ashore in the barge of the States of Holland, gay with pennons. They stood on the dunes and watched the great fleet of thirty vessels weigh anchor, and, headed by the King's ship flying the royal standard, in a fresh gale and happy weather set sail for England.

Two days later the fleet arrived at Dover. The *Nazeby*, now renamed the *Charles*, came close to land in the early morning, but the King chose to breakfast on the ship of the same rations that were served to the sailors. Then, about midday, he made a gift of a thousand ducats to the ship's company for having brought him in safety to England, and prepared to land. A specially built brigantine was waiting to carry him, but, with a gracious gesture to Montagu, the King insisted on going in the admiral's barge. Accompanied by his brothers, the Dukes of York and of Gloucester, he was rowed to the landing place, where a great crowd of people stood to welcome him. It was nine years since he had been smuggled out of Shoreham, after running as a fugitive across half England. How different was his return! As he set foot on the shore a rich canopy was held above him and George Monck, general-in-chief of the land forces and the most powerful man in the kingdom, fell on his knee and kissed his royal master's hand. He immediately entered a state coach and drove towards Canterbury. On Barham Down he mounted his horse and rode through a great troop of noblemen, knights and other cavalry who awaited him in rich apparel. They were drawn up on his left hand in lines of three and, as the King rode passed, they bowed to him, kissed the hilts of their swords and flourished them above their heads, while a fanfare of silver trumpets was carried in the wind from the sea. Entering his coach again, with the dog of which he was so fond, he drove to Canterbury to stay with Lord Campden.

Tuesday, 29 May was the King's birthday, an appropriate day for his entry into London. The Puritan tradition prevented displays of magnificence, but there was much simple rejoicing. On Blackheath he was met by 'a kind of rural triumph, expressed by the country swains, in a morris dance with the old music of taber and pipe; which was performed with all agility and cheerfulness imaginable'. At South-wark he was received by the Lord Mayor and aldermen of London in a pavilion hung with tapestry. A banquet was served, and then the great company assembled in order of precedence to ride into the city. John Evelyn stood in the Strand and watched the procession—'a triumph of above 20,000 horse and foot, brandishing their swords, and shouting with inexpressible joy; the ways strewed with flowers, the bells ringing, the streets hung with tapestry, fountains running with wine; the Mayor, Aldermen, and all the Companies, in their liveries, chaines of gold, and banners; Lords and Nobles, clad in cloth of silver, gold, and velvet; the windows and balconies, all set with ladies; trumpets, music, and myriads of people flocking, even so far as from Rochester, so as they were seven hours in passing the city, even from two in the afternoon till nine at night'. As the King rode down Whitehall he found the members of both Houses of Parliament waiting to receive him and to kiss his hand. From

Henry VII's chapel at Westminster came the sound of the *Te Deum* sung in a solemn service conducted by four bishops. But what may have pleased him more was the greeting offered to him by the young ladies of the city. They petitioned the Lord Mayor 'to grant them leave and liberty to meet His Majesty on the day of his passing through the city; and if their petition be granted, that they will all be clad in white waistcoats and crimson petticoats, and other ornaments of triumph and rejoicing'.

The coronation of Charles did not take place for a year after his return but the interval was fully occupied by the transition from the austerity of the Puritan régime to the gaiety of a court influenced by many years of residence abroad. In September 1660 Londoners saw a full display of this continental magnificence when the Prince de Ligne arrived to congratulate Charles on behalf of the King of Spain. He came with a train of over two hundred attendants and servants in two English warships. He was carried up the Thames in the King's private brigantine and made a sensational landing at the Tower of London. Never before had such superb carriages and such fantastic costumes been seen in the sober streets of London, but all this was as nothing to the contrast visible when the King received the ambassador in the Banqueting House. The court was in mourning for the King's brother, the Duke of Gloucester, and against the royal purple of the King and the black of his great officers were set the peacock colours and fanciful designs of the splendid noblemen from Spain and the Netherlands. The King himself led the movement towards an elaborate and luxurious life. He set fashions in clothes and wigs, especially a remarkable jewelled dress in the Persian style, he played with his pet dogs, he was an inveterate theatre-goer, he enjoyed music and played the guitar, he loved elegant and precious things, such as the gold medal made for him by Philip Rotier with the portrait of his favourite, Frances Stuart, as Britannia. During his reign the great craftsmen flourished; the incomparable silversmiths; the bindings which go by the name of Mearne; the workers in stucco and wrought-iron; the makers of walnut furniture—all serving the purposes of the greatest of all English architects, Sir Christopher Wren, and all encouraged by a monarch who loved luxury and appreciated its fruits.

The taste and skill of these craftsmen was used to prepare for a noble coronation. In 1649 the regalia was 'totallie Broken and defaced'. Robert Viner, the famous goldsmith, was commissioned to replace the regalia, using the traditional forms as far as possible. A series of superb ecclesiastical vestments, of crimson and purple velvet heavily embroidered in silver and gold, was specially made. Triumphal arches, to remain in position for a year, were erected in the city. Evelyn, who had seen the masterpieces of Italy, reported that they 'were of good invention and architecture,

CHARLES II's ARRIVAL AT THE HAGUE

An Engraving by P. Philippe, after J. T. Vliet, from 'Relation en forme de journal'

In the possession of the author

THE BALL GIVEN TO CHARLES II AT THE HAGUE ON HIS DEPARTURE

A Painting by Hieronymus Janssens at Windsor Castle

Reproduced by gracious permission of His Majesty the King

with inscriptions'. The King carefully revived the ancient ceremonials. On 19 April he created sixty-eight knights of the Order of the Bath. Evelyn went to the Painted Chamber at Westminster to see the ceremony, but bad weather deterred Pepys. This was the last occasion on which the knights were ritually bathed. Three days later there was another last occasion. The King rode in procession from the Tower to Whitehall, since when this portion of the ceremony laid down in the *Liber Regalis* has been discontinued. Pepys watched the procession from a window in Cornhill. It was a brave show, in which refinement laid a steadying hand on luxury. The liveries of the footmen were 'handsome, though not gaudy'. The dresses of the noblemen expressed the glory of the day. 'Embroidery and diamonds were ordinary among them.' The Knights of the Bath were 'in crimson robes, exceeding rich'. The King preceded by the royal sackbuts and cornets playing Matthew Locke's stately processional music, rode in a rich embroidered suit and cloak. Pepys found that his weak eyes were dazzled by the show of gold and silver, so that after a time he was not able to look at it.

The next day, 23 April, the King went by water to Westminster Abbey and was crowned with ancient ceremonial on a great scarlet dais raised before the altar. The crowd was so vast that most of the people saw nothing except the procession of the new regalia, and the noise was so great that Pepys 'could make but little of the musique; and indeed, it was lost to every body'. But many more, both in the Abbey and in the dense crowds outside, saw the King go on foot, wearing the silver crown imperial and carrying the gold sceptre surmounted by an amethyst globe, from the place of coronation to Westminster Hall for the banquet. His path was covered with blue carpet. He walked under a canopy of cloth of gold supported by six silver poles, carried by barons of the Cinque ports all dressed alike in crimson satin. At the corners were silver gilt bells which flashed and tinkled cheerfully as the King went through the afternoon sunshine. In Westminster Hall there was great pageantry and feasting; the Knights of Bath, in their robes, carrying the first course to the King; the heralds leading favoured guests to bow before the throne; the three great officers of state, on horseback, introducing the service of each course, and eventually bringing in the King's Champion, 'all in armour on horseback, with his spear and targett carried before him'. Three times he flung down the gauntlet and then rode towards the King's table. His Majesty drank to him and then sent him the gold cup. He drank it off and, holding it aloft, rode backwards from the hall. Gay music was played by twenty-four violins of the King's band, dressed in scarlet tunics.

At last the King rose to leave, and this was the signal for disorder both outside and inside the hall. The weather, which had been 'very serene and fair', changed suddenly to a terrible thunder-storm, the worst for many years, 'which people did take great notice of'. When the barons of the Cinque ports tried to carry the canopy to the King, it was seized by some of the royal footmen, and an unseemly scuffle took place. Eventually the King left and went by triumphal barge to Whitehall. Pepys stayed on the roof until it was late, expecting to see the fireworks devised by Martin Beckman, the famous Swedish fire-master. But, as the rain continued, there was nothing but bonfires.

In the year before the coronation there had been gossip as to whom the King would marry. Pepys was told that he was already married to the niece of the Prince de Ligne. But two weeks after his coronation the King summoned the council to announce to them his intention of marrying Catherine of Braganza, sister of Alfonso, King of Portugal. This princess was twenty-three years of age, of very retiring disposition, having seldom been outside the royal palace, following a life of rigid formality under the iron rule of her mother, the Queen-Regent. She was a Catholic and could speak no English. It was evident that such a bride for the pleasure-loving Charles must be bringing a great dowry with her. Such was the case. England secured Tangier and Bombay, trading privileges in three continents, and the promise of two million Portuguese crowns. The fact that the money was paid only in sugar and spices seems of small importance compared with the riches which flowed from the territorial gains. Edward Montagu, now made Earl of Sandwich for his services in bringing the King from the Netherlands, was appointed ambassador to conduct the princess to England. As one of Charles's most experienced admirals he was appointed to receive the surrender of Tangier on his way to Lisbon. He sailed on 13 June but contrary winds and affairs at Tangiers delayed him, and it was nine months later that he arrived at Lisbon to conduct Catherine to England. He landed on a beautiful spring day amidst the rapturous excitement of the inhabitants. Not only was their princess to become a great queen, but the value of the match was already abundantly clear. At the approach of the English fleet the Spaniards had called off their attacks on Portuguese territory. Surrounded by the joy of the common people and the punctilious politeness of the courtiers, Sandwich remained a month at Lisbon, being received by King Alfonso, 'a very fool almost', having distant audiences with Catherine, and bargaining with the Queen-Regent.

On St George's Day a solemn procession passed through the great palace over-looking the Tagus. The journey to England had commenced. Catherine, followed by her brothers, the King and Don Pedro, said farewell to her mother on the staircase leading to the chapel. She passed out into the streets she had so seldom seen and drove under arches of flowers, through crowds dancing around her coach, to the cathedral. Here a benedictory mass was held. The English emissaries, being Protestants, heard the florid music from the cloisters. Then the royal procession made its way through the gardens of the palace to the water-side. The ladies protected themselves from the sun with fans, as a barge, flying the Portuguese royal standard, carried the princess to the *Royal Charles*. On the quarterdeck the King handed her into the safe keeping of Lord Sandwich, but the bewildered lady attempted to follow her brother to the head of the companion-way and had to be ordered back for disregard of convention. They were ready to sail, but the wind veered and prevented them. That night there was an improvised display of great beauty. The city was illuminated, and a water carnival was held on the Tagus. Hundreds of little boats rowed out and threw up a glittering show of fireballs. The next day the wind was still contrary, so, to please his sister, the King came in the evening with musical courtiers in barges to serenade her. They floated under the gilded galleries of the great ships, plucking their guitars, while the ladies, clustered high above them, gazed down through their mantillas.

The crossing was tempestuous and Catherine suffered much. She remained in her inner cabinet, her only pleasure being to hear Lord Sandwich's music. The fleet ran for shelter to Mount's Bay and then followed the coast to the Isle of Wight. Each night the princess could see fireworks from the shore shooting into the sky to greet her. On 13 May, in warm, still weather, the *Royal Charles* dropped anchor, and the private barge of the Duke of York came alongside. Catherine received him in her state cabin standing under a canopy before a throne. In his honour she was wearing English dress of white cloth trimmed with silver lace. The Duke saw a lady 'low of stature, prettily shaped', with 'languishing and excellent eyes'. He greeted her in Spanish on behalf of his brother, and, though she replied only through her almoner, the way in which she stepped forward to meet him and her grave and gentle bearing made an impression that was not effaced during the thirty years she lived in England. The next day the combined fleets sailed up the Solent to Portsmouth. The Princess landed in a dress that was the extreme of Portuguese fashion, with a monstrous farthingale, a huge ostrich feather, and her hair arranged in pyramids of cannon curls. She was greeted by the Mayor and Corporation below the Sally Port and driven in a gilded state coach to the King's House.

The King did not hasten to Portsmouth. It was said that he was delayed by Parliament. At last he prorogued the House on 19 May and left that night by a fast coach for Guildford. He was accompanied by his cousin, Prince Rupert, and attended by a troop of Life Guards. The next morning he continued his journey to Portsmouth, where he found Catherine in bed with a feverish cold. There was speculation as to whether the wedding would have to be postponed, but the Princess awoke better in the morning. She insisted on being married first according to the rites of her own church, but, as the knowledge of this would have caused mischief in the country, the ceremony was conducted privately in her bedchamber by Lord Aubigny, one of her chaplains. In the afternoon the Protestant ceremony took place in the Presence Chamber before a magnificent company of nobles and their ladies. Catherine wore an English costume of rose-coloured silk, trimmed with knots of blue ribbon. It was noticed that she did not speak but signed her consent. When Charles led his Queen to his own apartments, Lady Suffolk cut the blue knots from the dress and distributed them as souvenirs. Catherine had not fully recovered. She retired early to her own room, where the King joined her at supper. In the other rooms of the house and throughout Portsmouth there was much feasting and entertainment.

The royal party did not leave immediately. Charles said that there was not sufficient transport for the *guarda infantas*, the gigantic farthingales of 'the Portugal Ladies'. But by 27 May all was prepared, and the state retinue set out for Hampton Court. Charles and Catherine rode in the royal coach, canopied and fringed but not glazed. People crowded the Portsmouth road to see them pass, the King in his Garter robes and the Queen in an English dress with her hair uncovered to show her wonderful coiffure. They broke the journey at Guildford and Windsor, encountering some difficulty with the ladies of Catherine's suite, who were so nice that they would not occupy beds that men had ever slept in. On 29 May the great procession reached Hampton Court. Clarendon, the Lord Chancellor, with the councillors of state, the judges and the ambassadors, were waiting to receive the new Queen in the rose-coloured Tudor palace. That evening, while bonfires blazed on the river banks, the Duchess of York came up the river from London in her own fine barge with many rowers, to pay her respects. These were the first of many formal visits which brought the fashionable world to see the Queen and her ladies, with 'their complexions olivader; her ceremonious courtiers; the great Indian cabinets, brought from Portugal, 'such as had never before been seen here'; the rich gondola with its gondoliers sent as a gift by the Signory of Venice; the Queen's musicians, harps, pipes and singers, performing the strange, rhythmic music of her country; perhaps even to receive from Catherine a gift of 'a gilded glassfull of perfumed comfits'.

Hampton Court became a corner of a foreign world, a fragment of the life the

THE ARRIVAL OF THE PRINCE DE LIGNE AT THE TOWER OF LONDON

A Painting by François Duchatel at Belœil (Photograph: A.C.I., Brussels)

Reproduced by courtesy of His Excellency the Prince de Ligne

[43]

THE PRINCE DE LIGNE PRESENTING HIS SON TO CHARLES II AT WHITEHALL
A Painting by Gilles van Tilborg at Belœil
Reproduced by courtesy of His Excellency the Prince de Ligne

CHARLES II IN HIS CORONATION ROBES
A Painting by J. M. Wright at St James's Palace
Reproduced by gracious permission of His Majesty the King

Queen remembered at Lisbon. She needed this small consolation in a world that would have seemed alien under the best conditions. It was against this background that her triumphal entry into London was arranged. In beautiful weather on 23 August the King and Queen were rowed downstream in the royal barge. At Putney they changed into a state barge so large that it could not go farther upstream. Evelyn saw them sweep down the river with twenty-four oarsmen, 'in an antique-shaped open vessel, covered with a state, or canopy, of cloth of gold, made in form of a cupola, supported with high Corinthian pillars, wreathed with flowers, festoons and garlands'. From Chelsea to Whitehall the state barges and water pageants of the City companies thronged the river, so that Pepys, standing on the roof of the Banqueting House, 'could see no water for them'. It was. said Evelyn, 'the most magnificent triumph that ever floated on the Thames'. The King and Queen landed at the privy stairs and were greeted by the Queen-Mother, Henrietta Maria. To Catherine this was more than a formal greeting; it was a welcome from a lady who shared her longing for another country, her love of a religion which was hated by the English, her deep sense of loneliness. In the Queen-Mother's palace at Somerset House, made by Inigo Jones into one of the most sumptuous residences in Europe, Catherine was to find friendship and understanding.

CATHERINE
OF BRAGANZA

A Painting by Dirk Stoop
National Portrait Gallery

THE DEPARTURE OF CATHERINE FROM LISBON AND HER ARRIVAL AT LONDON

Two Engravings by Dirk Stoop

THE PROCESSION OF THE ORDER OF THE BATH
An Engraving by J. Pine, after J. Highmore
British Museum

The Creation of The Most Honourable Order of the Bath

1725

. . . Nor shall, with Scaeva, Knights of Bath expire,
But unborn Heroes, proud, that name acquire;
That name in hallow'd Rites, and pompous Dress,
That name in Tilts, and Tournaments profess.
Ensigns of Dignity, the solemn Day,
The slow Procession, and the crowded Way,
Thro' a long Train of Centuries, yet unroll'd
With Pride, and Pleasure I at once behold.

LAURENCE EUSDEN, The Origin of the
Knights of the Bath; a poem, 1725

The Creation of The Most Honourable Order of the Bath, 1725

AT THE FIRST QUARTER of the eighteenth century the peaceful fortunes of England were guided by the firm hand of Robert Walpole. Although the great Whig statesman continued in office for another seventeen years, there were few moments when his prestige stood higher in both royal and popular favour than in 1725. The danger arising from the panic in South Sea stock had been averted; the Jacobite cause had not recovered from the defeat of 1715; England was not involved in the wars that ravaged the continent, and she had even succeeded in making a treaty with France and Prussia; the government pursued a policy of consolidation, and there was prosperity in the land—some part of all these satisfactory conditions was due to Walpole. It was natural, therefore, that when he suggested to George I that an honour should be granted to powerful supporters of the Whig party, the King took up the project enthusiastically and decided not only 'to re-establish and support' the Knighthood of the Bath but to erect it into a regular military order. Evidence was produced that the Order was founded by Henry IV at his coronation in 1399 and that knights had been created at each coronation up to the reign of Charles II. It was suggested that the true origins of knighthood by bathing were lost in the mists of antiquity, and that the King was proceeding to revive one of the ancient orders of chivalry. But John Anstis, who, as Garter Principal King of Arms, must have had much to do with the ceremonies in 1725, wrote that it was not easy to see how any learned man could ever infer that the Knights of the Bath had their commencement at the time of Henry IV, as knights strictly of a military order.

If the early history of knighthood by bathing is obscure this is only part of the greater obscurity of the origins of knighthood itself. It seems likely that the first conception of ceremonial to accompany the admission of young men into the ranks of warriors is to be found in Germany. Tacitus records such ceremonies as existing among the German tribes of his day. Similar customs then passed to the Franks of Gaul, where they were considerably developed. Charlemagne is known to have girded his son, Louis the Pious, with the sword when he arrived at manhood, as Louis later girded his own child, Charles the Bald. Some simple form of knighthood seems to have existed in England before the Norman conquest, so that Norman *chevaliers* were met by Anglo-Saxon knights. It was, evidently, one of the movements towards order and dignity which rose independently and simultaneously in many countries, as the pattern of life gradually became more complicated. It was not, perhaps, until after the Crusades that knighthood added to itself the strong religious inspiration now commonly associated with it. From very early times two ways of conferring knighthood existed in the countries in which chivalry was known. In both these the essential rite was the accolade or stroke of the sword, and, in the form used in time of war, this constituted the whole, or at least the greatest part, of the ceremony. But in the less hurried times of peace, there was opportunity for the 'courtly and sacred' ritual by which a heightened significance is given to the great occasions of public life. The ceremonies were courtly in the sense that there were feasts, music and the giving of robes, arms and spurs at the creation; they were sacred by virtue of the ritual of cleansing which preceded the dubbing.

The curious details of this ceremony are recorded in several ancient manuscripts. The process of inauguration began in the evening, when the squire was placed in the care of two governors. Under their direction, a barber shaved his beard, 'rounded' his head, and made ready a bath, 'in the best wyse that he can'. Then the King would command his chamberlain to go to the squire, accompanied by the wisest and worthiest knights and preceded by minstrels singing and dancing. When the governors heard the sound of music approaching, they undressed their master and put him into the bath. In solemn silence the knights entered the chamber and initiated the squire into the ideals of knighthood. When they had finished their exhortations, they poured a little water on his shoulders, and so departed. The governors were to take the squire out of the bath 'and ley him softly in his bed, to drye'. Later he was to rise, dress himself in a hermit's black garment, and be conducted with music and dancing to the chapel, where he was regaled with wine and spices before being left alone, to watch and pray 'tyll the dawnynge wex clere, and the Day come'. The night-long vigil in the chapel, lit by a solitary taper, emphasized the austerity which was one of the ideals of knighthood. After the celebration of Mass he was taken to his bed and permitted to rest, and while he slept his governors placed upon him a covering of cloth of gold. The symbolism was complete. The colours, even the materials, of the garments, had mystical significance; the whole ceremony was rich with allegory.

The earliest recorded occasion of a creation by bathing since the Conquest appears to be that of Geoffrey, son of Count Fulk of Anjou, who, being betrothed to the daughter of Henry I, King of England, was knighted by Henry at Rouen in the year 1128. Similar ceremonies are recorded as having taken place during the reigns of King John, Henry III and the Edwards, the third of the name being knighted five days after his coronation. From this creation dates the practice of placing the knight's armorial ensigns in the room in which he is bathed. At the coronation of Henry IV forty-six knights were created with such splendid and solemn ritual that the tradition grew that the King had founded an Order of the Bath. 'On Saturday before the coronation, the new king went from Westminster to the Tower of London, with many followers; and all the Esquires who were to be made knights the next day, to the number of forty-six, watched all that night, each of whom had his chamber, and his bath, in which he bathed; and the next day the Duke of Lancaster made them knights at the celebration of mass, and gave them long green coats with straight sleeves, furred with miniver, after the fashion of Prelates; and the said knights had on the left shoulder a double cordon of white silk, with tassels hanging down.' From this time onwards knights were created in this fully ceremonial manner at all coronations, and thus originated the practice of naming them Knights of the Bath. They were allowed precedence before knights bachelor, but their only distinction was that they had been knighted with more elaborate ceremonies than others, and on certain great occasions.

During the fifteenth century it became the custom to knight the sons of the monarch at an extremely tender age. This may have derived from the creation of Henry VI, who was knighted at the age of four. One of the youngest of these princes was Henry, Duke of York, afterwards King Henry VIII, who was only three years old when he was knighted by his father. George I determined to continue this custom when he 'revived' the Order and so he named his four-year-old grandson, Prince William, the third son of the Prince of Wales and, later, the Duke of Cumberland, as 'the first, and principal Companion'. This was only one of many steps the King took, not only to revive the Knighthood of the Bath, but to create 'a Brotherhood, Fellowship, or Association of a certain Number of actual Knights; subjected under a Sovereign, or Great Master, united by particular Laws and Statutes'. This act of creation was conscious and artificial to a much greater extent even than Charles II's revival of the Knighthood in 1661, when the honour was conferred on the unusually large number of sixty-eight knights. Much of the solemn spirit of the ritual had been lost by the break with tradition during the Commonwealth, and was replaced by more social ceremonies. Over sixty years were to elapse before anything more was heard of the Knighthood and then George I's creation of the Order followed the Caroline tradition rather than the Plantagenet.

On 18 May 1725 George I 'did erect the Degree of Knighthood by the Bath into a Military Order for ever', and at the same time he appointed John, second Duke of Montagu, to be its first Grand Master. Five days later he ordained the statutes of the Order and named the thirty-five Companions other than the Sovereign, a Prince of the Royal Blood and the Grand Master. On 27 May, in his closet in St James's Palace he conferred the degree of knighthood on his infant grandson, striking him with the sword of state and placing the red ribbon, to which the badge of the Order was affixed, over his shoulder. His Royal Highness kissed His Majesty's hand. The other Companions were then knighted.

On 17 June the ceremony of installing the elected knights took place. It is by no means certain that the rituals of bathing and keeping vigil were performed in accordance with ancient custom, although their execution was commanded in the new statutes. It is known that Prince William was granted a dispensation, 'since, by reason of the Tenderness of his Age, he is not able to bear the Fatigue of bathing, and the Vigils attending it', and that the Duke of Montagu was similarly absolved because of his office. The chronicler of the event contents himself with saying that all things necessary were prepared. Early on the morning of the seventeenth, in the Speaker's Chamber in the House of Commons, the knights invested themselves in robes based to some extent upon traditional dress. They wore surcoats of red, edged and lined with white, white girdles, stockings and gloves, long mantles of red, lined with white and fastened about the neck with lace of white silk. Each carried in his hand a remarkable tall white hat, topped with a splendid crest of white ostrich-feathers. Prince William, because of his youth, did not walk in the procession, and his place was taken by Sir Andrew Fountaine, his tutor, who wore his tall hat during the first procession but carried the child's mantle upon his arm. Sir George Saunders and Sir Chaloner Ogle, acting as proxies for the Duke of Richmond and Lord Glenorchy, both carried the mantles of their principals on their right arms.

At about ten o'clock in the morning, the company repaired to the Prince's Chamber in the Palace of Westminster, the Chapter Room of the Order, where the long procession formed, and whence it slowly set out. It was an impressive sight. At the head were the drums of His Majesty's Household, with kettle-drums and trumpets. Then came twelve almsmen of the Church of Westminster, followed by the Messenger of the Order, and the Knights' Esquires, wearing short white mantles,

PRINCE WILLIAM OFFERING HIS SWORD TO THE DEAN

An Engraving by J. Pine, after J. Highmore

British Museum

lined with red, red stockings and red bonnets of Tudor style. These were followed in turn by the Prebendaries of the Church of Westminster, the Pursuivants of Arms, and then the Knights Companions themselves, walking two by two. Next came the officers of the Order, preparing the way for the Grand Master in his full habit 'and with the Collar of Gold, compos'd of several Imperial Crowns, tyed or linked with Knots of Gold, representing the white Laces mentioned in the antient Ceremonials, weighing thirty onces of Troy-weight, having the Badge or Symbol of the Order thereto pendent'. Alone at the end of the procession walked Sir Andrew Fountaine, the last of over one hundred persons who wound their way solemnly through St Margaret's Churchyard. They went by a railed-in and carpeted passage-way skirting the Abbey, their robes and feathers flashing scarlet and white against the grey walls, their monstrous white hats giving them the appearance of giants moving through the crowd of spectators. At the West Door they entered and passed slowly from sight into the gloom of the great building.

The pageantry attracted considerable attention and, in their excitement, people of fashion used every means to obtain access to the Abbey. A few days before the ceremony the church was 'but one intire piece of Scaffolding', and in this way many places were provided, but Mrs Cadogan, Sir Hans Sloane's daughter, in her impatience to obtain a seat, wrote to the Duke of Richmond during his convalescence. 'I am persuaded, you have good nature enough to consider the consequence of missing a new show and the unfashionable thing it wou'd be, added to the curiosity and impatience incident to my sex.' Amongst the privileged spectators were the Prince and Princess of Wales, and their daughters, intent upon watching the deportment of little Prince William at his first public ceremony. Through this great throng of noblemen and ladies the brilliant company proceeded slowly up the length of the dark Abbey and disappeared into Henry VII's Chapel at the east end of the building. Here only a handful of onlookers could be seated. The procession mounted the steps into the Chapel and passed from the sombre shadow of the Abbey into the coloured light pouring from the great windows. Against the crisp fan-tracery of the carved rood the sumptuous figures commenced an elaborate ritual of choreographic intricacy, full of formal gestures and patterned movements. First entered the twelve almsmen, walking two by two; they bowed to the altar and to the sovereign's stall, then parted to stand in two rows, extending from the altar-rails. The Messenger entered, bowed, and took his place below the almsmen. Then came the Esquires, three by three, bowed and stood before their respective seats below the stalls of their Knights. The Prebendaries followed in twos and went up inside the altar-rails to assist in the ceremony.

After them came the Pursuivants and Heralds, who took up their positions below Prince William's stall. In a brilliant order of white and scarlet robes, the Knights themselves then entered; first the two knights in the lowest stalls passed up to the top of the Chapel, bowed in the middle of the choir, and withdrew to their places, followed by all the others in pairs. Attending them were the officers of the Order, the Register, the Gentleman-Usher of the Scarlet Rod, Bath King of Arms, and the Dean. The Grand Master walked alone, and, after him, Sir Andrew Fountaine, now accompanied by his principal, Prince William. His mother, the Princess of Wales, had carried the child in her chair to the Abbey, where he arrived in time to take his place in the climax of the ceremony. Wearing his mantle and collar and with his plumed hat on his head, he proceeded immediately to his stall and sat down. Thereupon, the service began.

Bath King of Arms made his double reverences in the middle of the choir and turned to the Grand Master, who returned the obeisance, before going to his stall, bowing twice again, and seating himself, wearing his great white hat. The King of Arms then repeated the formality with all the Knights in pairs, with the difference that they took their seats with their heads uncovered. The Grand Master, assisted by the King of Arms and the Gentleman-Usher, proceeded to the ritual of installation. Each knight was handed a transcript of the statutes. The Dean administered the oath, while Bath King of Arms held the Book of the Gospels. Then Bath handed the collar of the Order to the Grand Master, who put it about the neck of the Knight, placed the white hat on his head and caused him to be seated in his stall. The Knight immediately rose again and made his double bow, after which the Grand Master embraced and congratulated him. The Knight then sat again. So the unhurried and continuous rhythm of installation continued, until all the Knights were admitted to the companionship and were all seated wearing their hats.

When this ceremony was finished, and the Grand Master took his seat again in his stall, the Dean went to the altar and celebrated Divine Service. The white hats were then raised and placed on cushions before their owners. When the music played the first phrase of the offertory, 'Let your light so shine', Bath King of Arms rose and bowed to all in turn, commencing with the junior Knights. Then all, in the same order of precedence, rose, bowed and stood beneath their banners in honour of the Principal Companion, the young Prince, who moved towards the altar, bowing as he went. At the altar-rails he knelt and placed his oblation in the vessel held by the Dean. After he had returned to his stall, bowed and seated himself, all the Knights made their offerings in turn, escorted to the altar by Bath and the Gentleman-Usher.

THE KNIGHTS AT DINNER

An Engraving by J. Pine, after J. Highmore

British Museum

When the service was over the hats were replaced for the ceremony of offering the sword. Prince William was conducted to the altar-rails, where his sword was unsheathed for him and offered naked to the Dean, who restored it with the words, 'I exhort and admonish you to use this Sword to the Glory of God, the Defence of the Gospel, the Maintenance of your Sovereign's Right and Honour, and of all Equity and Justice, to the utmost of your Power.' When Colonel Paget, who had unsheathed the sword for the Prince, offered to sheath it again, the child said, 'No, for I'le put it in my self'. The other Knights then moved to the altar in turn, to offer and receive back their swords. The long and intricate ritual was nearing its completion; the Prince left the Chapel, Sir Andrew Fountaine took his place again, and the procession reformed in the same order as before. It moved through the Abbey and out into the afternoon light. But outside the West Door each Knight was accosted by the King's Master-Cook, in linen apron and with chopping-knife in hand. To each he said, 'Sir, you know what great Oath you have taken; which if you keep, it will be great Honour to you; but if you break it, I shall be compelled by my office to hack off your Spurs from your Heels'. There were two light showers of rain and the Knights returned to the Chapter Room a little more swiftly than they had gone.

At four o'clock in the afternoon another procession was formed, and the Knights made their way to the Court of Requests to celebrate their installation in a state dinner. The Companions, still adorned by their plumed hats, sat on one side of a long table, the officers of the Order, with Garter King of Arms, sitting at another table at the lower end of the room. The Principal Companion sat at a small table of his own, but he did not partake of the banquet. When the second course was reached, the music stopped playing, and Bath King of Arms rose, bowed, and proclaimed the style of Prince William, then that of the Grand Master, and so on for all the rest of the company. After the Prince had risen with his hat in his hand when his name was called, he was taken home to bed. The banquet continued, from *Crabbs Fierct*, *Trouts Marronated* and *Lobster Italiana*, through *Turky's with Bamboe* and *Geese Stuffade*, to *Pyramids of Sweetmeats*. But everyone was not pleased; one of the Esquires of the Duke of Richmond wrote two days later to his invalid lord, 'The entertainment at Westminster I think was hardly equall to the rest of the solemnity, tho very great.'

The long day of 17 June 1725 ended with a 'splendid collation' and a ball given at the Opera House in the Haymarket and organized by the Swiss impresario, John James Heidegger. The expenses were paid by the new Knights, and about seven hundred of the nobility and gentry of both sexes were offered a cold supper of lavish generosity. The tables were piled with crawfish, Westphalia hams, venison pasties, salmon, wild fowl, chickens, lobsters, fruit of all kinds, ice-cream, blancmange, jellies, cream, syllabubs, and trees of iced fruits. Before the ball started, Thomas Hill, another of the Duke of Richmond's Esquires, wrote, 'The whole has been performed with the greatest magnificence hitherto, and what remains they say will be the utmost stretch of Heidegger's invention.' His invention ran to the skilled organization of gay and extravagant masquerades, to which the revellers went in fancy dress to dance and to gamble. Heidegger had taken over the management of the Opera House from McSwiny in 1711, and by 1717 the masquerades were in full swing. At first they

A KNIGHT'S COLLAR AND A KNIGHT'S STAR
Engravings by J. Pine, after J. Highmore
British Museum

took place in the Long Room adjoining the theatre but soon they were held in the theatre itself, when the pit and stage were transformed into a great hall, lit by innumerable candles and lined, of course, by the boxes, full of excited spectators. Behaviour on these occasions was expansive, and in 1724 seventeen bishops combined to petition the King that he should put an end to such undesirable entertainments. The masquerades were, however, frequently patronized by royalty, and the only effect of the bishops' protest was that their name was changed to ridottos. The ball for the Knights of the Bath, probably more decorous than its predecessors, gave infinite pleasure to those who attended. Thomas Hill, writing two days afterwards, said, 'As for the ball, it was answerable to the former part of the day and the expecta-tions every body had raised to themselves from the knowledge of Heidegger's capacity. Never was so large an entertainment so wel disposed, with so much elegance of taste as wel as profuseness of materials. In short, to give you as high a notion of it as is possible, it far exceeded the best entertainment any masquerade had ever produced in that place.' The Duke of Richmond's Esquires left the theatre between three and four o'clock in the morning, when the entertainment had still some hours to run.

Thus a ceremony which began as something of an anachronism, dignified but pretentious, bringing together elements of ancient ritual from an age of chivalry to 'revive' an Order which had never existed, ended in a whirl of robust gaiety and enjoyment, which was authentic and of its period. The creation served its purpose. Several times revised, the Order now exists in dignity and honour, and is acquiring from time a genuine antiquity. Robert Walpole was justified, although he did not himself long remain a Companion. His witty younger brother, Horace, did not fail to pass a comment: 'He (Robert) meant to stave off demands for Garters, and intended that the red should be a step to the blue: and accordingly took one of the former himself.' In 1726, Robert Walpole, more firmly fixed than ever in royal and popular esteem, was admitted a Knight of the Most Noble Order of the Garter.

MEDAL OF PRINCE WILLIAM IN THE
ROBES OF A KNIGHT OF THE BATH
Designed by John Croker
British Museum

The Shakespeare Jubilee, Stratford-on-Avon

1769

. . . putting the 'Stratford Guide-Book'
under my arm, as a pillow companion, I
went to bed, and dreamt all night of
Shakespeare, the jubilee and David Garrick.

WASHINGTON IRVING, The
Sketch Book of Geoffrey
Crayon, Gent

The Shakespeare Jubilee, Stratford-on-Avon, 1769

BY THE SPRING of 1769 David Garrick had been acting for twenty-eight years. During the greater part of that time he had been the acknow-ledged master of the English stage. Even his critical friend, Dr Johnson, admitted that he had 'long reigned the unequalled favourite of the public'. It was a position which exposed him to the bitter shafts of envy. He was accused of vanity, but, although he was hurt at the coolness of George III's applause when he performed before him privately, in most ways he bore himself with moderation. He was accused, too, of avarice, but at the same time there were those who reproached him with luxury, sneering that he lived as a prince rather than as an actor. Throughout his career he had found his greatest successes in the plays of Shakespeare. In the twenty years during which he built up his repertoire he had acted seventeen Shakespearian parts. He frequently presented the plays in recklessly garbled versions, but, in his own expression, he never let Shakespeare out of his hands or his pockets. He became the poet's champion and even carried his effective advocacy across the Channel into the intellectual circles of Paris, giving demonstrations which proved at least a balance to the rival theories of the great Voltaire himself.

When, therefore, the Coporation of Stratford-on-Avon was building a new Town Hall and wished to have a statue of Shakespeare to adorn a niche on the north side, there was no one to whom they were more likely to turn than the famous actor-manager of Drury Lane. The story, as it has so often been told, is full of the pettiness of local politics. The facts are that, in May 1769, a delegation from Stratford visited Garrick in London and presented him with a box, carved from the wood of Shakespeare's mulberry tree, containing a document making him the first honorary freeman of the borough. Garrick, pleased at the honour, returned his official thanks in a courteously worded letter and at the same time privately intimated his intention of presenting a leaden statue of Shakespeare by Scheemaker, a version of the figure in the Poets' Corner at Westminster Abbey, and a painting of 'Shakespeare in his Study' by Benjamin Wilson. Stripped of insinuations of unworthy motives on both sides, these are the events from which grew the first celebration of Shakespeare in his native place.

The season at Drury Lane closed on 23 May and Garrick immediately left for Stratford to discuss with the burgesses a proposal to celebrate the opening of the new Town Hall by a festival in honour of Shakespeare. The suggestion was approved and Garrick accepted the office of Steward. The date fixed for the opening was 6 August and plans were made for a summer festivity. In *The London Magazine* of May, the first of several incongruities was committed—the festival was announced as Shakespeare's Jubilee, a name which even the kindliest critics considered 'rather inaccurate'. Garrick enlisted the help of a group of proved assistants: Latimore, to design and erect the amphitheatre; French, the scenic artist at Drury Lane, to paint the transparencies, some of them based on designs by Sir Joshua Reynolds, which decorated the river bank, the new Town Hall and Shakespeare's birthplace; Domenico Angelo, the famous fencing master, to devise the firework displays and the lighting effects which were so remarkable a feature of the transparencies; and his faithful brother, George Garrick, to supervise the business arrangements.

The amphitheatre, rotunda or Jubilee booth, as it was variously called, was an elegant, octagonal building, erected on the Bankcroft near the river. Its design was based on that of the fashionable rotunda at Ranelagh. The interior was supported by a circular colonnade of Corinthian columns and lit by a magnificent chandelier of eight hundred lights. Between the pillars were hung crimson curtains. The walls and ceiling were rich with gilt ornaments and painted decorations. It held a thousand spectators, with a special space for a hundred musicians. Not a single person, standing in this exquisitely designed circle, with the light from hundreds of candles flashing from cut glass on to gold and crimson, could believe that it was all built of wood and that within a few days it would be demolished. Not only was its life so short but the memory of it faded swiftly too. It seems that no picture of the interior was painted but it may not be fanciful to believe that more than a hint of its appearance is to be found in Robert Adam's drawing of the Fête Pavilion which he designed at The Oaks, Epsom, in 1774. Here is a similar ballroom, with gilded frieze and painted ceiling, enclosed within a circle of handsome pillars.

The finest of the transparencies, that taken from the designs of Reynolds, was used to decorate the set-piece of the fireworks. This was erected on the other bank of the river, opposite the amphitheatre, with the intention that the fireworks should be seen reflected in the water. The painting represented Time leading Shakespeare to Immortality, supported on each side by Tragedy and Comedy. At the Town Hall five windows were decorated with transparencies, Shakespeare in the centre, with Falstaff and Pistol on his left, and Lear and Caliban on his right. At the Birthplace there was an allegorical transparency of the sun struggling through clouds to enlighten the world. The lighting effects for these transparencies were invented by Domenico Angelo, who, although he was by profession a fencing master, was an ingenious man who frequently proved his usefulness to Garrick. He was one of the great actor's links with the more spectacular theatre of the continent. As a young man at Venice he had seen moving scenery, transparencies, and actors appearing in black silhouette. When he came to London, he invented a toy theatre on these lines to please the royal princes who were his pupils. Garrick immediately engaged him to teach the use of these mechanical devices to French, the scene-painter at Drury Lane. He held strong views on the subject of theatrical costume and was a skilful arranger of firework displays. He was Garrick's adviser in all the departments needed to make this festivity a success and it was in his house in Carlisle Street, Soho, that the details of the Jubilee were planned.

While Garrick and his friends were making their elaborate preparations, the people of Stratford were considering what they could do to entertain the crowds that were expected. There was some hesitation, even some active hostility, not surprising in view of the novelty of the event, but in spite of these difficulties arrangements were made to cater for the arrival of fashionable visitors in the little country town. The proprietor of the White Lion Inn almost doubled his accommodation. He built a large assembly room, a card room, a coffee room and a small suite of private apartments for the use of Mr and Mrs Garrick. He ordered three hundred dozen pewter plates, knives and forks, a hundred dozen pewter spoons, fifty dozen stewpans and ten pipes of wine. He engaged three hundred waiters. The Corporation fitted up the fine Elizabethan house adjoining the derelict site of Shakespeare's New Place as a lodging for the High Steward, the Duke of Dorset. A Chinese summerhouse was erected on the terrace over the Avon. Cooks were hired, hairdressers came, sedan chairs were brought from Bath and London. A masquerade warehouse

THE STATUE OF SHAKESPEARE AT THE
TOWN HALL, PRESENTED BY GARRICK
An Etching by R. B. Wheler, 1803
Trustees and Guardians of Shakespeare's Birthplace

was opened in Chapel Street, where it was intended that the nobility and gentry should select their dresses. In the midst of so much activity it was inevitable that hitches should occur. The lamps to give coloured light for the transparencies, sent in two large wagons from London, arrived broken; work on the amphitheatre was held up for lack of timber; there was friction between the local workmen and the stage carpenters brought from Drury Lane. But the main difficulty was lack of time. It was found impossible to complete the arrangements for a festivity on this scale in a little more than two months. The date was altered by a month and the opening fixed for Wednesday, 6 September.

During the preceding weeks thousands of people flocked to Stratford to see the buildings and decorations being erected. Even the visitors arrived a week or ten days before the opening, to make sure of their lodgings. The streets were congested with carriages and overrun with horses. Transport was a serious problem. The Angelo family failed to get post horses from London to Oxford, where they had an engagement to sup with the Garricks *en route* to Stratford. The climax of the preparations in London was reached at the chilling hour of four in the morning on Saturday, 3 September, when the musicians and actors set out in a grand cavalcade from Mr Pritchard's in Oxford Road. They travelled in ten coaches and four, and six post chaises, with a number of mounted gentlemen riding beside them. Actors and musicians, setting out to ride into the heart of England to the first celebration of Shakespeare—they must have been a merry company! But the people at Stratford, watching the rain falling day after day and the river rising dangerously near the new amphitheatre, must have had gloomier thoughts.

At dawn on 6 September the opening of Shakespeare's Jubilee was announced by the firing of thirty cannon on the banks of the Avon and the beating of the *Reveille* by the fifes and drums of the Warwickshire Regiment of Militia. Immediately the stream of pleasure began to flow and it did not pause for nearly twenty-four hours. Young actors from the theatre, fantastically dressed, serenaded the ladies as they prepared for the day's festivities. They sang to the accompaniment of hautboys, flutes, clarinets and guitars. Through these pleasant sounds Garrick made his way from the Mayor's house, where he was lodging, to the new Town Hall. Here the

JAMES BOSWELL IN THE DRESS OF AN
ARMED CORSICAN CHIEF, AS HE APPEARED
AT THE SHAKESPEARE JUBILEE
An Engraving by J. Miller, after S. Wale
British Museum

A PRINTED COTTON HANDKERCHIEF WITH SCENES RELATING TO THE JUBILEE, *c. 1769*

Trustees and Guardians of Shakespeare's Birthplace

Town Clerk, on behalf of the Mayor and Corporation, formally invested him with the emblems of his office as Steward of the Jubilee. These, a portrait medal of Shakespeare set in gold and a wand, both made of the famous mulberry tree, he wore throughout the celebrations. His first task was to receive the company at a public breakfast held in the Town Hall. He was pleased to see that many had responded to his printed appeal that they should make their dresses gay by wearing the beautiful jubilee ribbon which had been specially woven at Coventry. As he looked around him he saw hundreds of favours, rosettes and sashes of this rainbow-coloured silk. Many of the visitors had added to this the excellent portrait medal of Shakespeare engraved by Westwood, which had been specially struck in gold, silver and copper, to suit all classes. As they sat at breakfast and the corps of drums and fifes played outside, Garrick was able to inspect the company for the first time. His strong social instinct must have been gratified when he saw two dukes, six earls and almost as many countesses, a good sprinkling of other peers, with baronets, knights, members of parliament and prominent landowners. But, with his delight in intellectual company, perhaps he felt some disappointment when he saw that from his circle of intimate friends only Macklin, Foote, Colman, Murphy, Mr and Mrs Yates and young Boswell had made the journey. And even with several of these he had had sufficient experience to suspect that their presence was due to a desire to tease him. Garrick was a sensitive man and would show signs of irritation at the jealousy of Macklin and Murphy even when he was at the height of his fame. But the sharpest thorn in his side was Samuel Foote, a mimic of genius, who, from his stage at the Little Theatre in the Haymarket, satirized the foibles and fashions of the town. The sight of him, stumping about Stratford on his wooden leg, must have caused Garrick much misgiving.

But the celebrations were crowding after each other too swiftly that day to allow time for nervous anticipations. The company proceeded to the church, where Dr Arne conducted a performance of his oratorio, *Judith*, with the beautiful Mrs Baddeley, Mrs Bartholemon and Vernon, one of the finest tenors of the day, amongst the soloists. This was the second of the strange incongruities of this event. *Judith* was a successful oratorio, its composer was an old friend of Garrick and a frequent butt of his good-humoured mimicry, but no one could see why it should have a place in a Shakespearian festival. Some of this bewilderment was forgotten while Garrick did homage at Shakespeare's grave and bust, decorating them with garlands of flowers and evergreens. Then the Steward of the Jubilee headed a procession from the church to the amphitheatre. Most of the visitors walked behind him but the nobility rode in

their coaches. As they moved, and afterwards at the rotunda, Vernon led the chorus in lively songs specially composed by Arne and Dibdin. At three o'clock the visitors, six or seven hundred of them, sat down to 'a sumptuous public ordinary', prepared by Payton, of the White Lion Inn, with the help of his imported cooks and army of waiters. They ate turtle and venison and later drank tea or coffee before they retired to their lodgings to prepare for the evening assembly.

The weather, although it was not ideal for a festival of procession and pageantry, had remained fair throughout the day. While the visitors were resting and changing, Domenico Angelo, his heart full of memories of the pompous *Bucintoro* on the canals of Venice, and of ducal celebrations against the warm night sky of Italy, was inspiring his assistants to transform this grey and green little town into a place where glittering coloured lights threw into velvet shadow the dark lanes running to the river, where the quiet, old-fashioned houses would look fantastic in the reflected flash of fireworks. It was a hard task, in which the English weather, the English landscape and the English temperament gave little help. But the transparencies were bright with scarlet, crimson and pale blue lights, bonfires were blazing. Clitherow, the pyrotechnist from Ranelagh Gardens, was ready in Angelo's set-piece. Drums were beating in the streets and, as darkness fell, the crowds moved towards the amphitheatre. Light from its great chandelier splashed on to the river bank and the band was playing a minuet. At a prepared moment, perhaps when the minuets and cotillons gave place to country dances, the soaring of rockets signalled the commencement of the fireworks. If the company which crowded from the rotunda expected to see all the display on the ornamental screen on the opposite bank they received a pleasant surprise. The ingenious Angelo had built three small turrets on that portion of the bridge which is reflected by the Avon. Along the parapet now ran blazing serpents. When they reached the turrets they revolved within them and darted back again along the bridge. All this concluded with a large sun on the top of the transparent and illuminated building, with six *pots d'agrets*, an elaborate form of Roman candle, and a flight of six dozen sky rockets. About three in the morning the last country dance was played, the last lights dipped and the weary revellers went home through dark and echoing streets.

The second day began as had the first, with firing of cannon, ringing of bells, serenading of ladies and public breakfasting. But it can hardly have begun again at dawn. Not even the sprightly Garrick could rouse himself so early after so late a night. When he emerged, gashed by a tired and nervous barber, he found that the rain had come again and that the river was rising rapidly. A hasty council was held, and Lacy, his partner at Drury Lane, refused to permit the theatre costumes being used in the Shakespearian pageant planned to take place that morning. The pageant was postponed and the visitors made their way through the rain to the rotunda for the performance of Garrick's *Ode upon Dedicating a Building, and Erecting a Statue, to Shakespeare*, with interspersed airs and choruses composed by Dr Arne. Scheemaker's statue was nobly erected at the back of the orchestra. Before it, dressed in a suit of brown silk embroidered with gold lace, sat David Garrick. Around him were grouped the musicians, under the direction of the composer. Garrick was conscious that this performance was the heart of the festival. His great abilities responded to this act of dedication. His talent as a poet was not great. His *Ode* was sharply criticized when it was published but, as it was heard that wet September morning by a thousand people in a draughty amphitheatre, it seemed superbly worthy of the occasion. Boswell said that Garrick seemed in ecstacy as he declaimed it. It was received with a wild enthusiasm which frequently interrupted the performance and at the end there was general agreement that honour had been done to the supreme dramatist by the supreme actor. Dr Arne's share was not forgotten; indeed it has had a more permanent life, as the exquisite air, *Thou softly flowing Avon*, recognized at its true worth at the first performance, is still enchanting listeners nearly two hundred years later.

The fine effect of the performance of the *Ode* was achieved in spite of the absence of the spectacular climax which Garrick had planned. The pageant, consisting of one hundred and seventy performers, some of them actors from the London theatres, representing the principal characters in Shakespeare's plays, should now have entered and crowned the statue with a wreath of laurel. The 'dozen of the handsomest children in ye town', whom Garrick had chosen from the local schools as fairies, were disappointed but still hoped the pageant would take place the next day. In its place was some rather tedious speech-making, which Garrick tried to enliven by using King, the famous comedian, dressed as a *macaroni*, to attack the fame of Shakespeare. This sophisticated device puzzled some of the audience and led to dissatisfaction. But the excitement occasioned by the collapse of a portion of the seating, followed by the arrival of a monstrous turtle for dinner, put everyone in good humour again. They ate and they sang, and then they went home through the rain to prepare for the masquerade ball.

The warehouse in Chapel Street had been open for days, hiring out costumes at four guineas each and upwards. At the inn and in the lodgings an eastern potentate donned his rich robes, witches huddled into their rags, Shakespeare's ghost stalked again, and a shepherdess looked at herself in the mirror and was pleased. And every-

where was the badge of folly, the Venetian mask. Garrick and Angelo, when they planned this ball, had dreamed of warm nights on the Piazza, of a scrap of black lace across sparkling eyes, a hood of white velvet over a handsome head, moonlight and music. Now, as they looked out, they saw rain pouring down in torrents, the river overflowing its banks, turning the low-lying land around the rotunda into a marsh, they heard the fizzle of damp fireworks. But, as midnight approached, a thousand people struggled through the rain to the ball. Horses waded knee-deep in water as they approached the amphitheatre. Planks were laid from the entrance to the floors of carriages, to enable ladies to alight. It was the worst flood in the history of Stratford. But inside the rotunda there was light, music and supper. And especially there was the surprise provided by young James Boswell. Moved by admiration for Paoli, the Corsican patriot, he appeared as an armed Corsican chief, in a dark coat and scarlet waistcoat and breeches. In his black bonnet he had a blue feather and cockade and across the front, embroidered in letters of gold, the motto *Viva la Libertà*. He carried a stiletto, a pistol and a fusee, and in his hand was a vine staff, with a bird carved at one end, an emblem of Shakespeare. He pulled from his pocket a long poem in praise of Corsica and Shakespeare and would have read it to the company. But they had heard enough poetry for one day. They preferred to dance, to peep beneath the masks, and to watch Mrs Garrick, the exquisite Violetti who had delighted connoisseurs at the Opera twenty years before, dance the minuet with incomparable grace.

The weather was a little better on Friday but it was still too wet in the morning for the postponed pageant to be given, so the performance of the *Ode* was not repeated. Many of the visitors did not wait for the Jubilee Gold Cup horse race. They looked at the swamp around the rotunda and decided to go home. To a depleted company Garrick made his final bow and yielded up the emblems of his stewardship, while the band played the farewell dance and the last rockets shot into the sky.

The echoes were a long time dying. Garrick staged the pageant at Drury Lane and made it one of the most splendid successes of his career. Foote threatened to satirize him at the Haymarket and then, with one of his rare flashes of geniality, made peace with him. Scheemaker's statue was erected in its niche on the Town Hall and stands there to this day. A sadder fate attended the picture by Wilson and the superb portrait of Garrick by Gainsborough, which the corporation of Stratford bought to commemorate the Jubilee. They were both destroyed in the fire of 1946. Garrick's memory lingered in the little town. When Washington Irving was there fifty years later, the sexton told him he remembered Garrick, 'a short punch man, very lively

GARRICK RECITING THE ODE
An Engraving after J. Lodge

In the possession of the author

VIEW OF THE AMPHITHEATRE AND FIREWORK SCREEN
A Watercolour Drawing by James Saunders

Trustees and Guardians of Shakespeare's Birthplace

and bustling'. One echo would have rolled on even longer, if Samuel Johnson had been there to start it. Alas! he was at Brighton with the Thrales. The man who could say of Garrick, when he performed before the King, 'Sir, he should not, in a Royal apartment, expect the hallowing and clamour of the One Shilling Gallery,' and only two years later write, 'I am disappointed by that stroke of death, which has eclipsed the gaiety of nations, and impoverished the public stock of harmless pleasure,' that man would have had much to say about the Jubilee, both as to its folly and its splendour.

GARRICK AS STEWARD OF THE JUBILEE
An Engraving by Saunders, after Van der Gucht, 1773
Trustees and Guardians of Shakespeare's Birthplace

The Coronation of George IV

1821

I am glad that the Pavilion still stands here in Brighton. Its trite lawns and wanton cupolæ have taught me much. As I write this essay, I can see them from my window. Last night, in a crowd of trippers and townspeople, I roamed the lawns of that dishonoured palace, whilst a band played us tunes. Once I fancied I saw the shade of a swaying figure and of a wine-red face.

MAX BEERBOHM, King George the Fourth
(*Works:* John Lane The Bodley Head, 1896)

KING GEORGE IV AND HIS TRAIN-BEARERS
A Drawing by J. or F. P. Stephanoff

Victoria and Albert Museum

The Coronation of George IV, 1821

WHEN GEORGE III DIED on 29 January 1820, after reigning for nearly sixty years, his eldest son and heir, the Prince of Wales, succeeded to a title which he had held in fact if not in name for nine years. It was in 1811 that the old King's insanity could no longer be concealed. His son was made Prince Regent, and proceeded to rule the country on principles very different from those of his father, whose popularity, based on the decorum of his private life and the sturdiness of his public actions, was strong with the middle classes. The Prince of Wales had reacted against the strict austerity of his parents' life; he was handsome and well-informed; he had a taste for music and the arts; he swiftly became a leading figure in the world of gaiety and fashion. When he was only fifteen his tutor predicted that he would be 'either the most polished gentleman or the most accomplished blackguard in Europe—possibly both'. The truth of this double prophecy was borne out, on the one hand, by his notorious behaviour towards his wife, and, on the other, by the favourable impression he made on people of discrimination. In his paradoxical make-up elements of good taste and flamboyance, intelligence and stupidity, generosity and selfishness, were constantly at war, with the result that he attracted to himself not only the company of prize-fighters and profligates but also that of the poets and finest minds of his time. Amongst all the outrageous gossip that has gathered around his name, it is good to remember that Sir Walter Scott recorded that he possessed the rare and enchanting 'art of raising one's spirits', and thought him 'the model of a British Monarch'.

From 1811 the Prince ruled uneasily but ostentatiously. His father was still alive at Windsor, completely cut off from knowledge of the world. His wife, from whom he was separated, removed herself to Italy and commenced the eccentric life that eventually brought about the final clash. His only daughter, Charlotte, to whom he tried to show affection in his strange way, married in 1816 and died in childbirth next year. His good looks were bloated by self-indulgence. His taste, formerly curbed by an economic rein, now galloped into the wildest extravagances of fashion. His days were filled with planning and enjoying the additions of a golden drawing-room, a Gothic dining-room and a black and scarlet vestibule at Carlton House; with driving in his bright yellow curricle to see the building of a thatched cottage *orné* in Windsor

Great Park in 'a habit of unspoiled magnificence'; with travelling in his private sleeping coach to Brighton to watch the flowering of his fantastic bulbous Pavilion; with forming his royal band, at a cost of six thousand pounds a year; with eating the vast but elegant meals provided by his chef, the great Carême; with creating the incredible collection of wardrobes full of once-worn suits of silk and plush, satin and doeskin; with playing gracious host to visiting sovereigns and gossiping vivaciously with Sheridan, Byron, Major Hanger and 'Beau' Brummell; with patronizing an army of artists who would record his appearance, decorators who would make the luxurious *objets d'art* he loved, and architects who would alter the face of London. The results of his failings crowded close upon him. He was forced to importune Parliament to pay his debts. But he was stupendously alive, and, through his extravagance, the whole country burgeoned with exotic growth.

When the news came that the Regent was King at last, he was desperately ill. A cold he had caught at Brighton had turned to congestion and only the most violent bleeding saved his life. As soon as he recovered, he returned to London to consult with the Cabinet about the problems raised by his accession. Foremost amongst these was the question of his wife's position. He refused to allow prayers for the Queen to be admitted into the liturgy. The Cabinet were not happy about this and recommended that the Queen's annuity should be paid only during her residence abroad, hoping, by this means, to avoid the embarrassment of her presence in the country. The Queen answered the implied accusation by setting out for England. Henry Brougham, one of her chief advisers, was sent to negotiate with her, but she did not wait for him and crossed to England on 5 June. The country was stirred uneasily by these developments, and popular feeling was running against the King. A great crowd went to Greenwich to meet the Queen on 7 June on her way to London. Amongst them was Charles Greville, who recorded that ' "Her business," as they call it, will in all probability raise such a tempest as they will find it beyond their powers to appease'. Throughout the summer the legal and political wrangle continued. The King was at Royal Lodge and was virtually barred from his capital. It was impossible to think of a coronation in such circumstances, especially as the King had announced that Caroline would be excluded from the ceremony. In October he forced a reluctant Government to bring in a bill to divorce the Queen and to deprive her of her royal title. It was fought with the utmost violence, not only in Parliament but throughout the whole country, and, when the third reading had a majority of nine votes only, it was abandoned by the Government.

The King accepted his defeat and set about regaining his popularity. On two successive nights in February 1821 he went to the theatre for the first time since his accession. At both Drury Lane and Covent Garden he was received with immense acclamations, only a few people showing signs of disapproval. A man in the gallery called out, 'Where's your wife, Georgy?', but this was almost drowned by the cheering from the pit. Although the King affected to despise the opinion of the mob, his favourable reception encouraged him to proceed with arrangements for his coronation. He next took the advice of Lord Gwydyr as to the attitude of the dandies. When he was told that they were not well disposed towards him, he explored the possibilities of winning their favour, as they were not only a social but a political force. It was decided to invite them to a state breakfast in the House of Lords on the morning of the coronation, and in this way their opposition was overcome. The King's anxieties in connection with his wife were by no means at an end. From the continued activities of her lawyers it became certain that she would claim her right to be present at the coronation, but in the decision not to admit her the King was strongly supported by the Government. He was still nervous. First, the date of the coronation was fixed for 12 July; then it was altered. Eventually, Thursday 19 July was selected, and the preparations began in earnest.

To a monarch who loved splendour and extravagance, a coronation was an opportunity to indulge in a ceremony of dazzling magnificence. The Gothic Revival was in the ascendant. It was natural that the King, who admired the mediæval poems of Scott and possessed a Plantagenet conservatory in cast-iron at Carlton House, should desire to have a coronation that would bring back the spirit of ancient chivalry. In every one of a thousand details the desire to revive old traditions was expressed. The first of these was the choice of the Pontifical of Egbert as the coronation service. This, the most ancient ritual of crowning known in English history, had been used only once since the fourteenth century, at the joint coronation of William and Mary. Costumes believed to have been used at the coronation of Henry VIII were copied for the Harbinger and other officers. The uniform of the Yeomen of the Guard had a genuine antiquity, at least as far back as the reign of James II, but the lace cravats worn with the deep-skirted coats did not give a sufficiently 'Tudor' appearance to the eyes of George IV, and they were therefore substituted by ruffs. In this way was created the attractive but anachronistic costume worn by the Yeomen to this day. One of the most chivalric of the ancient ceremonials, the service of King's Champion, received the King's closest attention. It was to be performed in its full glory, as though a premonition warned him that this picturesque survival of feudalism would be swept away at William IV's 'half-crownation' and would never be revived. But the mediæval influences did not outweigh other considerations. The King, still uncertain of his public reception, did not revive the gorgeous and significant procession from the Tower to Westminster on the day before the coronation. He did, however, retain the pre-coronation enthronement in Westminster Hall, the procession on foot to the Abbey, and the return to the Hall for the coronation Banquet.

Nothing occupied the King's attention more carefully than his own garments— 'his profusion in these articles was unbounded'—and, especially, the regalia he would use. He chose the length of crimson velvet embroidered with golden stars, for his train; the black Spanish hat, with a spray of white ostrich feathers surmounted by a black heron's plume; the wig of thick, falling curls; the dress of silver tissue, trimmed with silver lace, *à la Henri Quatre;* and the superb crimson velvet robe, studded all over with the rose, the thistle and the shamrock. The expense and design of the regalia made by Rundell and Bridge, the court jewellers, were the cause of prolonged negotiations. An Imperial State Crown was made at a cost of £70,000 but as the Prime Minister would not sanction its purchase, the jewellers quoted £7,000 for its hire and included jewels which brought its value to more than double the original price. There was a delay in deciding whether it should be bought, with the result that the fee for its loan was increased to nearly £18,000. Jewels to the value of £100,000 were hired for St Edward's Crown, which had been dismantled after the coronation of William and Mary. The jewellers were reluctant to lend so many precious stones for this crown, and pointed out that they would be locking up too much stock at a time when it was most saleable. The Sword of State, which still exists, is probably the most intrinsically valuable weapon in the world. It is heavily encrusted with diamonds but its brilliant effect is obtained by the emblems of England, Scotland and Ireland in coloured gems on the hilt and scabbard. There was a circlet of brilliants for His Majesty's cap of state, six coronets for the Royal dukes, four coronets for the Royal duchesses and princesses. The crown jewellers, court tailors and dressmakers accepted the immense burden of work imposed by such lavish preparations, but the King himself directed the whole scheme. An eye-witness recorded that 'the most minute attention must have been bestowed to arrange all the subordinate parts in harmony with the rest'.

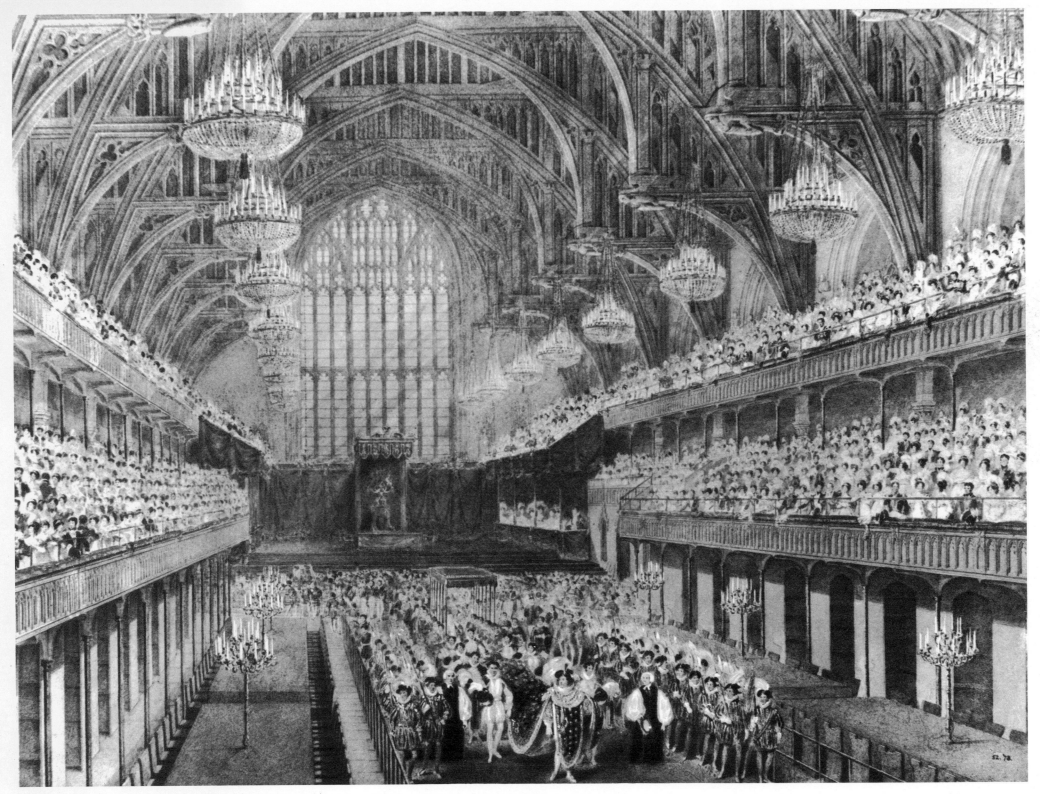

THE PROCESSION FROM WESTMINSTER HALL TO THE ABBEY

A Drawing by Charles Wild

Victoria and Albert Museum

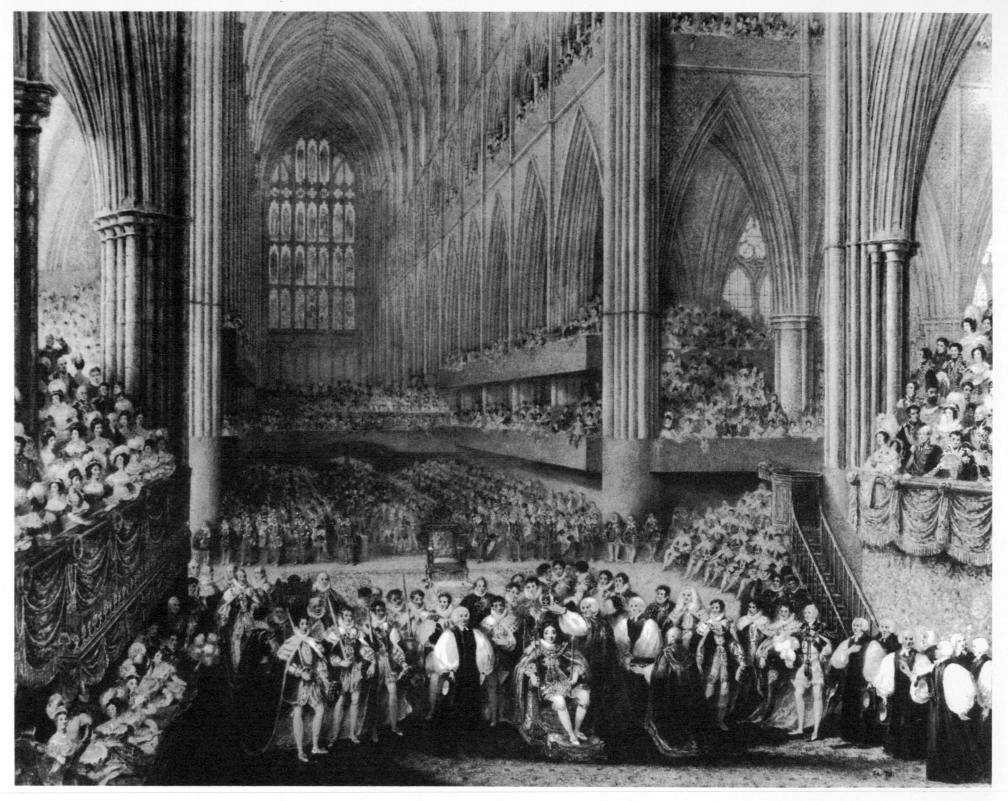

THE ARCHBISHOP OF CANTERBURY PLACING THE CROWN ON THE KING'S HEAD

A Drawing by A. C. Pugin and J. Stephanoff

Victoria and Albert Museum

At half-past eight in the evening of 18 July the King drove in a closed carriage from Carlton House to the Speaker's residence at Westminster. There he spent the night, but is doubtful if he was able to obtain much rest as the bells of St Margaret's rang and the guns on the park fired every half hour from midnight. The spectators, roused by anticipations of a pageant which would remain vivid for the rest of their lives, began to throng the streets at one in the morning. Everywhere along the route there were galleries called 'The Royal George' or 'The Ladies' Fancy', for those who could afford from two to twenty guineas a seat, but thousands of others stood wherever there was foot-space and listened to the noisy passing of the half hours in the mild air of the early summer morning. Ticket-holders were asked to be in their places by seven o'clock, so that there was soon a profusion of arrivals to engage the spectators' interest. But before that time they were witnesses of one of the most dramatic and pathetic incidents that has ever occurred at a coronation. At five o'clock Queen Caroline left her residence in South Audley Street and was driven in a coach of state drawn by six bays to Westminster. As she passed through the Green Park the news of her arrival spread, and thousands of people converged from all directions on Storey's Gate. The coach made its way slowly through the crowd of cheering and waving sightseers, until it stopped before Westminster Hall. The Queen, leaning on the arm of Lord Hood, attempted to enter, but she was informed that no person whatever could be admitted without a ticket. She tried two other doors and then walked to the House of Lords, with the same result. Returning to her carriage, she drove to the Abbey. Here Lord Hood enquired of the chief door-keeper whether any preparations had been made for Her Majesty. He was told that none had been made, and, amidst some jeering, the Queen re-entered her carriage and was driven away.

It was at Westminster Hall that the opening of the tremendous ceremonial was to be seen. The magnificent room had been transformed by tiers of wooden galleries, all draped; a scarlet and gold dais for the King; and a triumphal arch in the Gothic style, thirty feet high, with a gallery above it for the King's band. Benjamin Haydon, the painter, was at the Hall at half-past one, but three ladies were there before him. At four o'clock the doors were opened, and the ticket-holders were admitted. The scene was full of contrasts, at once stately and raffish; the peers strolling about in their fine robes; the disputes over people in seats they had no right to occupy; the sun lighting up the Gothic windows; the pugilists in charge of the doors getting tipsy and quarrelling amongst themselves—these and many other incidents combined to create an atmosphere of excitement and anticipation before the King made his

appearance. The tension was increased as ten o'clock, the hour announced for his arrival, came and went. The delay was caused by the Marquis of Graham, acting as the Lord Great Chamberlain, tearing his robes as he put them on. But the crowd knew nothing of this, and Haydon was conscious that 'a whisper of mystery turns all eyes to the throne. Suddenly two or three rise; others fall back; some talk, direct, hurry, stand still, or disappear. Then three or four of high rank appear from behind the throne; an interval is left; the crowds scarce breathe. Something rustles, and a being buried in satins, feathers, and diamonds rolls gracefully into his seat. The room rises with a sort of feathered, silken thunder. Plumes wave, eyes sparkle, glasses are out, mouths smile, and one man becomes the prime object of attraction to thousands. The way in which the King bowed was really royal. As he looked towards the peeresses and foreign ambassadors, he showed like some gorgeous bird of the East'.

In the distance a gun was fired on a man-of-war stationed in the river, and all the waiting crowds knew that the solemnity had commenced. The regalia was borne up the Hall by the Dean and Prebendaries of Westminster, laid before the King and then handed by the Lord Great Chamberlain to the officers of state whose privilege it was to carry the crown, the orb, the sceptre, the swords, the spurs and the staff to the coronation. The procession was formed and, as the choirs sang 'O Lord, grant the King a long life', it commenced the slow and stately journey to the Abbey. At the head of the long file came the King's Herb Woman, with her six maids, strewing the way with herbs and flowers. Their white dresses and their graceful movements made a vivid contrast to 'the unwieldy splendour of the Heralds, who glowed like huge masses of cloth of gold and silver' and the plumed magnificence of the Knights of the Bath. The King seemed oppressed with the weight of his robes and the heat of the day. Frequently he wiped his face, and an officer had to support him as he descended the steps of the dais. The immense train of crimson velvet, nine yards long, dragged at his shoulders, and he asked the eight train-bearers to hold it farther from him, to relieve him of the weight. But he talked cheerfully to the Bishop of Lincoln as the procession moved out of the Hall, and then in the full sunlight of a summer morning, he mounted the platform stretching to the Abbey and commenced the ceremony of 'offering himself to be seen by the people'. The platform was the structure on which the Royal procession passed to the Abbey and back again, raised so that the King could be seen by as many people as possible. The railing on each side of it was covered with purple cloth and nearly the whole of its great width was carpeted in blue. It was covered with an elaborate system of moveable awnings, the lines and pulleys of which were controlled by men in special livery stationed along the route. Protected by close lines of troops and great numbers of special constables, the King passed to the Abbey in the full view of his people.

The coronation ceremony was solemn and splendid, from his entry, as the choir sang the Hallelujah Chorus, to his departure five hours later, in the purple, gold and silver robes of Estate. During this time the King was often affected by heat and fatigue, but Sir Walter Scott recorded 'that he roused himself with great energy, when anything occurred which excited his personal and immediate attention'. This was especially noticeable when the Duke of York gave him the fraternal kiss, amidst the plaudits of the assembled company, and at the moment when the peers placed their coronets on their heads, and the Treasurer of the Household threw gold and silver medals among the congregation. The effect, said Scott, 'was really august'. But this grandeur was somewhat diminished during the King's absence of ten minutes to don his robes of Estate. 'As soon as His Majesty disappeared the throng began to crowd out of the church. When the King returned, he had empty benches covered with dirt and litter on the one hand, and the backs of his courtiers expediting their exits upon the other.' But George did not seem displeased and moved forward with great good humour. The return procession was not in such good order as it had been at the outset, but the open gates of Westminster Hall, two thousand lights burning within, and the promise of a great banquet, welcomed the weary and the hungry.

The herb-women again preceded the King. The Hall was becoming shadowy when they entered, although the sunlight could still be seen on the scarlet uniforms around the platform. Haydon, still eagerly observing the scene, after thirteen hours in the Hall, heard 'the distant trumpets and shouts of the people', and saw 'the slow march, and at last the appearance of the King crowned and under a golden canopy'. Amid the long line of his nobles, he passed to the dais. Sir Walter Scott noticed the extraordinary profusion of singular and colourful dresses. 'Separately, so gay a garb had an odd effect on the persons of elderly or ill-made men; but when the whole was thrown into one general body, all these discrepancies disappeared.' When the King was seated the first course of the banquet was served to him by a procession entering through the Gothic arch. The clerks of the kitchen and sergeants preceded three of the great officers of state, who, mounted on horses caparisoned with plumes and feathers, led in the Gentlemen Pensioners bearing the dishes. After the course was served, the three peers backed their horses from the Royal presence down the whole length of the Hall. Then followed the most imposing scene of all. The doors swung open, 'and outside in twilight a man in dark shadowed armour appeared against the shining sky. He then moved, passed into darkness under the arch, and suddenly Wellington,

Howard, and the Champion stood in full view, with doors closed behind them'. Scott, more prosaic than Haydon, said that Dymoke, the Champion, was 'a fine looking youth, but bearing, perhaps, a little too much the appearance of a maiden knight to be the challenger of the world in a King's behalf'. Others made fun of the archaic ceremony by saying that the white charger he rode was borrowed from Astley's Circus. But everyone agreed that he made a brave figure as he rode up the Hall, pausing three times while the herald proclaimed the challenge in a loud voice, and three times throwing down his gauntlet. The third time brought him to the steps of the dais. The King took a gold vessel from the cupbearer and drank to the Champion. Dymoke drank to the King from the same cup, made his obeisance, and backed his horse from the royal presence.

Then the peers rose and drank the King's health with three times three. As the ninth round of cheering died away, His Majesty replied, 'The King thanks the peers for drinking his health and does them the honour of drinking their health and that of his good people.' He then withdrew and entered a closed carriage to return to Carlton House. His feelings of uncertainty about his reception were not assuaged and he decided to return by a devious route. Lord de Ros, an officer in the Life Guards, offered his services and piloted the coach through the back streets and lanes of Westminster, while the King shouted for the pace to be hastened and for the escort to form up more closely about him.

The departure of the King was not unwelcome to the vast crowd gathered in the Hall. They were ravenously hungry, and now, at last, was it possible for the peers, the aldermen and the ambassadors to commence the gargantuan meal provided under the direction of Watier, the Clerk Comptroller of the Kitchen, and Benoit, the *patissier*, famous for his hot jellies. Nothing was provided for the peeresses or for those who had purchased seats in the galleries and who had now been sitting there for seventeen hours. One peer was seen tying a cold chicken in his handkerchief and throwing it to his son. Then the looting started. The uproar almost drowned the music of the King's band, playing under its famous leader, Franz Cramer. But soon the fatigue of this momentous day made the spirits of even the most vivacious begin to droop. Carriages were sent for, but many did not come to time or in the right order. The guests were exhausted; some dozed where they sat, but many more lay on the floor and slept. It was three o'clock in the morning before the last carriages could get away, and at that hour the ladies had to be carried to their conveyances. When the last weary reveller had gone, the Hall was left littered with the remnants of the banquet, under the flickering lights of a few candles.

MR CRAMER, LEADER OF THE KING'S BAND   GEORGE COLMAN, LIEUTENANT YEOMAN OF THE GUARD   MR WHATTIER, CLERK OF THE KITCHEN

STEPHANOFF'S DRAWINGS OF PEOPLE PRESENT AT THE CORONATION

Victoria and Albert Museum

THE KING'S CHAMPION IN THE BANQUETING HALL

A Drawing by Dighton at Windsor Castle

Reproduced by gracious permission of His Majesty the King

The Funerals of Nelson and Wellington

1806

The Lord reward brave Nelson, and protect his soul,

Nineteen Sail the combin'd fleets lost in the whole;

The Achille blew up amidst them all,

Which made the French for mercy call:

Nelson was slain by a musket ball.

Mourn, Britons, Mourn.

The Battle of Trafalgar
(A broadsheet poem)

1852

Lead out the pageant: sad and slow,

As fits an universal woe,

Let the long long procession go,

And let the sorrowing crowd about it grow,

And let the mournful martial music blow;

The last great Englishman is low.

TENNYSON, Ode on the Death
of the Duke of Wellington

NELSON'S FUNERAL PROCESSION
FROM GREENWICH TO WHITEHALL

An Engraving by I. Hill from a Painting by C. A. Pugin

The Funeral of Nelson, 1806

ON 21 OCTOBER 1805 the British fleet under Vice-Admiral Lord Nelson broke through the line of the combined fleets of France and Spain about seven leagues from Cape Trafalgar. H.M.S. *Victory*, with the Admiral on board, led the weather column in a daring raid into the middle of the enemy's ships, which were so closely clustered together that it was impossible for the British vessel to get through without running foul of one of them. Nelson knew this and held boldly to his course. The *Victory* passed so close to the French ship *Redoutable* that their yardarms became locked together. In this dreadful proximity the sailors fought, while Nelson walked up and down the quarter-deck with the short, brisk step his men knew so well. As he turned he was shot through the spine by a sniper in the mizzen-top of the *Redoutable*. He lingered for three hours in the dark and stifling cockpit, while the ship was shaken by the concussion of her own broadsides. The surgeon could do nothing for him; his only comforts were to be given sips of water and to be fanned. Before he died he knew that his brilliant plan had succeeded. The enemy's fleet was cut in two and fourteen or fifteen ships had surrendered. 'That is well,' he said 'but I bargained for twenty.' He clung to his authority to the end and when asked if Admiral Collingwood should now take command, he raised himself in his bed and exclaimed, 'Not while I live.'

The victory of Trafalgar was complete. The enemy's fleet was not merely defeated; it was destroyed. For over one hundred years no enemy threatened Britain's naval supremacy. But it was a victory won at great cost in men's lives, thousands being killed and wounded in the two fleets. The battle was the final proof of the skill and daring which made Nelson invincible, but, in the way in which the fleet responded to him, it was also the conclusive evidence of his power over the hearts of those he led. By his presence he inspired men to deeds beyond their normal compass, and they followed him, not only because they had faith in his incredibly sure judgment, but because he was able to make them share his own passion for England and the sea. In temperament and habits he was the least English of all great Englishmen, and yet, during the last two years of his life, when he was at the centre of the whole great drama that Napoleon was unfolding, and, even more profoundly, at the time of his glorious death, he seemed to his people the epitome of courageous and far-sighted patriotism.

The news of his death, said Southey, 'was felt in England as something more than a public calamity. It seemed as if we had never, till then, known how deeply we loved and reverenced him'. The King, who had often received him with coldness, expressed the surge of public feeling when he commanded a state funeral without waiting for the sanction of Parliament. The people needed to pay their last homage to the man who had given them so much, not only in his victories, but by increasing their faith in themselves.

Nelson's body was conveyed to England in the *Victory*, under the command of Captain Hardy, who had walked with him on the quarter-deck when he was hit. On 22 December the ship arrived at Sheerness. The body was transferred to a yacht and taken up the river to Greenwich, through lines of vessels with their colours at half-mast and between the forts of Tilbury and Gravesend, where minute guns fired throughout the journey. Nelson's coffin had been waiting for him for seven years. After the Battle of the Nile one of his captains had taken the main-mast of the French flagship, *L'Orient*, from the sea. He had instructed his ship's carpenter to make a coffin of it and then had presented it to Nelson, so that when the time came he would be buried in one of his own trophies. This gift made a strange appeal to the great commander. For some time he kept the coffin standing upright in his cabin, until his friends, distressed by this morbidity, begged him to remove it. One of his last actions before leaving London in September 1805 had been to instruct the undertaker with whom the coffin was stored to engrave its history on the lid. In this shell his body was now placed and the whole enclosed in an elm coffin. On Christmas Day he was carried ashore by sailors from the *Victory*. They placed the colours of his ship around him and bound them with a piece of rope. He was to lie in state in the Painted Hall at Greenwich Hospital but as the preparations were not yet complete, the coffin was placed in the Record Chamber until Sunday, 5 January.

An immense crowd had been gathering since early in the day and as soon as the gates were opened the people rushed violently in. With difficulty the gates were shut again and then reopened to admit people in batches of fifty. At the foot of the stairs leading to the Painted Hall the pressure was intense and sailors used boarding pikes to allow only a few to pass at a time. The Great Hall was completely hung with black draperies and was lit by wax candles in silver sconces. At the far end, within a semicircle of candles, stood the coffin covered by a rich and splendid pall. Only a few bright objects flashed in the light; his viscount's coronet on the coffin; some state ornaments at its foot; his coat-of-arms placed at the head; and the flags rising in spirals to the distant roof—the rest was engulfed in the simple darkness of mourning, an atmosphere which suited the mood of the people. They stood in thousands to enter the Hall. On the first day alone about twenty thousand had to leave without gaining admittance. The leaden coffin in which he was brought home was cut in pieces and distributed, 'as relics of Saint Nelson', said the gunner of the *Victory*. Crowds almost as great went to view the preparations in St Paul's Cathedral, and expressed indignation that a charge was made. Over a thousand pounds was said to have been taken; it did not seem appropriate to the memory of Nelson. On the third day the public were excluded for a time from the Painted Hall while the sailors and marines from the *Victory* were taken by Lord Hood to see their commander's coffin. At five o'clock the doors were finally closed, but there still remained two ceremonies in which to honour the great sea-captain.

On 8 January the body was conveyed to the Admiralty, on the first stage of its journey to St Paul's. At midday a signal gun was fired from a boat on the river and the procession assembled in the Painted Hall. Preceded by fifes and drums playing the Dead March in *Saul* and surrounded by the great admirals and his own men from the *Victory*, who had shared in his triumphs, Nelson was carried to the place of embarkation. He was placed in a funeral barge manned by forty-six seamen. The Lord Mayor, the members of the City companies, the admirals, all took their places in their state barges. It was flood-tide, but the wind blew down-stream. Slowly the sombre procession of boats, with their flags at half-mast, made their way up the deserted river. All the shipping had been cleared, and there were no sounds except the splash of oars and the dull thud of the minute guns at Greenwich. Thousands of people stood on the banks, watching in silence. For three hours they watched 'Nelson's funeral streaming up the Thames', until it approached the stairs at Whitehall. The state barges drew up in two lines, through which the funeral barge passed, while the gun-boats continuously marked the passing of the minutes. At this moment the sun disappeared behind a bank of black clouds, and there was a violent hailstorm. As the coffin was disembarked the clouds broke, leaving a fair sky under which the procession moved slowly to the Admiralty. There the body rested for the night, in the captains' room, attended by Nelson's chaplain, who had kept watch every night during the lying-in-state.

All night the streets sounded to the tapping of hammers, as, by the smoky flare of torches, labourers worked to erect stands for the onlookers. Long before the workmen had finished the first spectators came sleepily to their places. As the faint, early light revealed the infantry in close, double files lining the route from the Admiralty to St Paul's, vast throngs of people all wearing mourning, moved quietly into position. They packed every foot of the way, they climbed steeples and spires, they were silhouetted against the distant sky on the roof of the Opera House in the Haymarket. At eleven o'clock there was a roll of muffled drums, and the Duke of York, the Commander-in-Chief, rode out of the Admiralty. Following him came a procession that seemed to have no end. The carriage of the Prince of Wales, which followed the bier, did not arrive at Temple Bar until two o'clock in the afternoon. There the Prince paused, to allow the first carriages to draw up to the Cathedral. Those who stood near listened to the distant tramp as the long procession came on and died away, dimly seen in the mist of that January afternoon. The funeral car was drawn slowly up Ludgate Hill, carrying to every beholder a memory of the great battle which had occasioned this grievous loss. It was partly modelled on the hull of the *Victory*, the stern being carved and painted in naval style, with the name of the ship in raised letters on the lantern over the poop. It halted before the West Door of the Cathedral, and, to the solemn music of Dr Croft, sung by the choirs of St Paul's, the Abbey and the Chapel Royal, the coffin was carried to the great canopy under the dome. The congregation, terraced on stands in each archway, seemed to float into the upper spaces of the vast building. During the service darkness fell, and the coffin and the grave were illuminated by a great octagonal lantern, painted black and containing one hundred and thirty lamps. By its light six admirals covered the coffin with a black velvet canopy, crowned by six plumes of black ostrich feathers, and Garter King of Arms proclaimed the titles of the dead man, broke his staves of office and threw them into the grave. The flags of the *Victory* were then taken to be placed for ever with her great commander, but the men who had served under him and loved him were moved by an impulse so powerful that they forgot the stately pomp, the royal Dukes at the graveside, the thousands of onlookers towering into the gloom— they remembered only 'our Nel'. They rushed forward and seized the great flag. It was torn into shreds and every man had a relic, so that as long as he lived he could show it and say 'I served with Nelson'.

FUNERAL PROCESSION OF LORD NELSON FROM THE ADMIRALTY TO ST PAUL'S

An Engraving by M. Merigot, after A. C. Pugin, 1806

British Museum

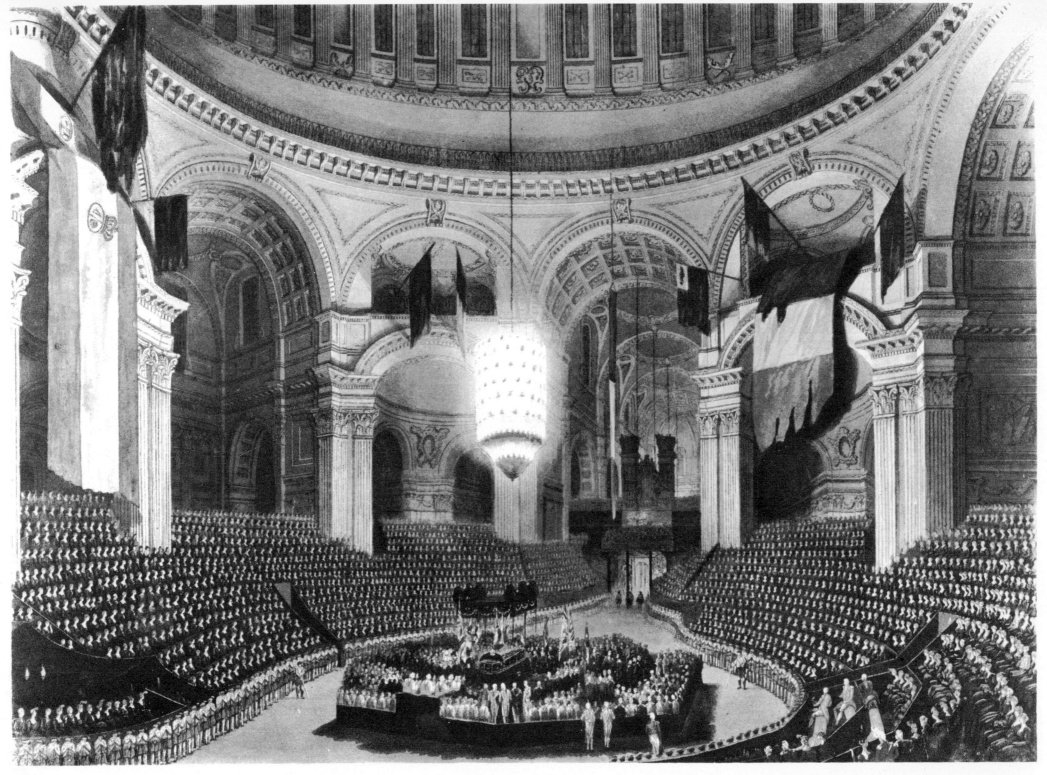

THE INTERMENT OF THE REMAINS OF LORD NELSON AT ST PAUL'S

An Engraving by F. C. Lewis, after A. C. Pugin

British Museum

LORD NELSON'S FUNERAL CAR
An Engraving by Ackermann, after McQuin
National Maritime Museum

THE DUKE OF WELLINGTON'S FUNERAL CAR
In the possession of the author

The Funeral of Wellington, 1852

THE DUKE OF WELLINGTON died quietly in his chair at Walmer Castle on 14 September 1852. He was eighty-three years old, and it seemed that a whole era died with him. It was not only that the poet laureate, in rather ponderous lines, begged Nelson to welcome his spirit—Nelson, his great contemporary, who had died nearly half a century before—but that his countrymen, from the highest to the lowest, had long regarded him less as a man than as a symbol of England's supremacy. To the Queen he was no longer 'the old rebel' but 'the *greatest* man this country ever produced, and the most devoted and loyal subject, and the staunchest supporter the Crown ever had'. The crowds who had broken the windows of Apsley House because of his resistance to the Reform Bill, remembered now only the great general who, until a few weeks before, had ridden regularly to the House of Lords in his cabriolet of highly personal design, wrapped in his white cloak, to sit through tedious hours of debate and to make, occasionally, a plain blunt speech. The Queen was right when she said that 'he was to us a true, kind friend and most valuable adviser'. Throughout her reign she had been accustomed to turn to him in problems of great difficulty, and he never failed to give mellow advice couched in brief, astringent phrases. The crowds cheered him by a sound instinct. They had heard he was a great soldier; they believed he was a judicious statesman, although he always supported established institutions; but they knew he was a remarkable 'character', simple in his habits, acid in his conversation, tender in his affection for children, wise in the conduct of his life. Few may have taken seriously the exaggerated sentiment of the Queen and her Poet Laureate that 'the last great Englishman is low' but everyone felt that, with the death of Wellington, two generations of English power had passed. Tomorrow the world might still be good but it would be different.

The Queen was in Scotland when the Duke died. She was sketching by a loch in the lonely hills when Lord Derby's letter was brought to her. She wrote in her diary, 'To *us* his loss is *irreparable*.' Immediately her thoughts turned to the possibility of a funeral that would express by its grave splendour the honour due to his memory. It was her desire to give directions for a public funeral as her grandfather had done at the time of Nelson's death but regard for democratic principles deterred her. Victoria

decreed that the Duke's remains should be guarded until Parliament met in November, in order that 'such honours should not appear to emanate from the Crown alone, and and that the two Houses of Parliament should have an opportunity, by their previous sanction, of stamping the proposed ceremony with increased solemnity, and of associating themselves with her Majesty in paying honour to the memory of one whom no Englishman can name without pride and sorrow'. In the meantime directions were given for the army to mark in a special way the loss of its great Commander-in-Chief. In addition to the usual mourning, officers on duty were ordered to wear a black crape scarf over the right shoulder, black crape over the sash, and black gloves. The Prince Consort wrote a memorandum: 'Victoria wishes the Army to mourn for the Duke as long as for a member of the Royal Family.' Albert had special reason to grieve. The Duke had shown confidence in him at a time when the Prince's position in England had not been easy. Only two years before he had asked Albert to succeed him as Commander-in-Chief. The Prince must have remembered that now, but it is unlikely that he regretted his decision to remain an adviser to the Queen.

The Duke's body was placed in a quadruple state coffin, the outer shell being made of Spanish mahogany covered with crimson velvet. At the head of the lid was a ducal coronet and at the foot a medallion of the Order of the Garter. This vast funeral chest, weighing nearly two tons, was placed in the simple room overlooking the sea in which the Duke had died. The camp bed on which he always slept and the few other pieces of austere furniture were removed, and the room was hung with black. Dominating the room on its velvet stand, the coffin stood there for nearly two months, watched night and day by a guard of honour from the Rifle Brigade. On 9 November the inhabitants of the Cinque Ports, of which the Duke had been Lord Warden, were admitted to the castle. All day long they thronged the beach, and filed past the plumed and candle-lit coffin. The next day the remains were taken, as privately as possible but not without salutes from the batteries at Walmer, Deal and Sandown, to London Bridge station and thence to Chelsea Hospital. There was a sense of fitness in the choice of a hospital for disabled soldiers as the setting for the lying-in-state, but there was a sense of contrast too. Wren's building, which Carlyle

THE DUKE OF WELLINGTON'S FUNERAL
PROCESSION PASSING APSLEY HOUSE

A Lithograph after L. Haghe

Guildhall Museum

considered 'quiet and dignified and the work of a *gentleman*', was transformed by Creekrell into an apartment befitting a funeral triumph. An observer noticed that the effect was 'not unlike that of the decorated shrines in Catholic cathedrals', but he had a superficial eye. The crowds who flocked there in hundreds of thousands for six days may have carried away little impression except the gloom of black drapery, the guttering of gigantic candles, and the brilliance of the silhouette of the coffin against its dais of cloth of gold. But perhaps there were a few visitors who made their way down a dimly lit corridor, and stood in the cool gloom of the vestibule under Wren's dome, and wondered. On one side stood the chapel, darkened and empty; on the other, the entrance to the Great Hall, guarded by a soldier in scarlet. Beyond the door it was no longer the hall but a black and silver tent, in which the hundreds of lights found no reflection and burned as single sparks in a great darkness, in which the sounds of the shuffling crowds had no echo but fell deadened on the ear. Concealed lights drew every eye to the crimson coffin on the gold dais, under a soaring canopy of black velvet lined with silver tissue. In the upper shadows of the tent were plumes of black feathers rising from silver sockets. This was no place of weeping; it was a scene of martial pomp—an apotheosis of victory by people who, blessed with a generation of peace, had forgotten the meaning of war.

Everyone, from the Queen to the costermonger, went to Chelsea. They assembled in vast crowds before the Hospital was open. On the privileged day thousands failed to gain admission; on the first public day there was a stampede in which two people were killed and dozens injured. The rain fell in torrents, and the crowds went dripping through the glittering darkness to the catafalque they had waited so long to see. It was still raining on the night of Wednesday, 17 November, when the coffin was withdrawn from its tent, and carried to the Horse Guards. All night it rained, but, in the dim light of early morning, as the troops gathered on the parade, it ceased. Grey clouds streamed across the sky, driven by a strong November wind. It was eight o'clock; the first minute gun sounded from the Tower, and the great crowds lining the streets knew that the funeral procession had started. The Queen was at Buckingham Palace, watching from a window. Nearly four thousand men marched in slow

AN IMPRESSION OF WELLINGTON'S FUNERAL CAR PASSING BUCKINGHAM PALACE
A Drawing by Queen Victoria
Reproduced by gracious permission of His Majesty the King

[92]

THE DEPARTURE FROM THE HORSE GUARDS
A Lithograph by Maguire

Guildhall Museum

[93]

THE DUKE OF WELLINGTON'S LYING-IN-STATE AT CHELSEA HOSPITAL
A Lithograph by W. Simpson, after L. Haghe, 1853
British Museum

THE CEREMONY AT ST PAUL'S
A Lithograph by W. Simpson, after L. Haghe, 1853
British Museum

time, with arms reversed, along the Mall. Melancholy thoughts crowded the Queen's mind. 'We shall soon stand sadly alone . . . Melbourne, Peel, Liverpool—and now the Duke—*all* gone.' The cavalry and artillery rode by, followed by a slow train of fifty coaches—judges, mayors, statesmen, admirals, company directors. The Queen saw the Prince Consort pass in a coach with six horses; the Duke's seven marshal's batons carried by generals of the countries whose wars he had done so much to win, and then his coronet resting on a black velvet cushion. The funeral music of the band of the Grenadier Guards grew louder, the minute guns thudded monotonously in the distance, and then the great allegorical chariot carrying the coffin was drawn before the palace by twelve black dray-horses. The original design had seemed supremely right to Victoria and her husband, and now the Queen hastened to make a swift sketch of it as it passed. Weighing eighteen tons, it was cast from bronze guns captured in the Peninsular war; it was modelled with emblems, trophies and heraldic achievements; it was hung with wreaths of real laurel; in the front was a trophy of real arms, prepared under the direction of the Board of Ordnance, from the collection at the Tower. The catafalque was hung with black velvet and silver lace. On it lay the coffin, high above the mounted men and protected from the weather by a delicate canopy of silk and silver tissue. The Queen said it was a beautiful sight.

This immense car, twenty feet long and seventeen feet high, rolled on, to pass the drawn blinds of Apsley House and to wind its way down through the Strand to Temple Bar. Here the halberds supporting the canopy were lowered by machinery to allow the car to pass through the arch. The representatives of the City joined the procession for the final stage of the journey to St Paul's. The Cathedral had been closed for weeks while suitable preparations were made. In the streets around, the crowds were so thickly packed that the lamp-lighters could not reach the street-

lamps, and they burned all day in the cold November light. Carlyle might think that the car was 'of all objects I ever saw the abominably ugliest'. Shaftesbury might lament these 'signs of mortality but none of resurrection . . . It was solemn, and even touching; but it was a show'. To the people who stood for hours in the damp streets it was that and something more. They watched bareheaded and not a sound was heard.

At the Cathedral the ambassadors of the great foreign powers were waiting—all except the Austrian representative. The Austrian uniform had been insulted in London when Marshal Haynau was seized by brewers' draymen and beaten. But Wellington was a field-marshal of the Austrian Empire, and a funeral parade was held in Vienna in the presence of the Emperor, when twelve batteries sounded the requiem of a great commander. Amongst the diplomats at the Cathedral was the envoy extraordinary of France, Comte Walewski. It was an ironical twist of time that he, a son of the Duke's old enemy, Bonaparte, should mourn him on the express instructions of Bonaparte's nephew, the Prince-President. It seemed that half Europe watched the procession, even as it was said that half England rode in it. But there was one omission. There was no representative of a section of the community for whom the Duke had peculiar affection. If he had been in charge of the arrangements he would certainly have noticed it. So, as the great ones of the earth in their rich uniforms followed the coffin into the cathedral, old Haydon the painter would have remembered an autumn day at Walmer when six children clamoured at the windows. 'Let them in,' said Wellington. They poured into the room with cries of 'How d'ye do, Duke? how d'ye do, Duke?' The old man hugged them, three a side. 'I want some tea, Duke' cried one urchin thirstily. Yes, old Haydon would have remembered, but he was dead too.

The Visit of Louis-Philippe, King of the French, to Queen Victoria

1844

Excepting a small tri-coloured cockade in his hat, he had nothing whatever in his dress to distinguish him from any other gentleman. He is a well-looking, portly, middle-aged man, with something of dignity in his step which, notwithstanding the unpretending citizen-like style of his promenade, would have drawn attention, and betrayed him as somebody out of the common way, even without the plain-speaking cocarde-tricolore.

FRANCES TROLLOPE, Paris
and the Parisians, 1836

LE DEBARQUEMENT A PORTSMOUTH
A Painting by E. L. G. Isabey at the Musée de Versailles
Musée de Versailles

The Visit of Louis-Philippe, King of the French, to Queen Victoria, 1844

THE CHARGE OF INHOSPITALITY so often levelled against the British appears to be based on imperfect evidence. It is true that our records of state visits do not glitter with the sumptuous entertainment of foreign monarchs, as do the archives of France and Italy, to the regret of those who believe with Bacon that such forms should not be despised. But in other and discreeter ways this country has not been found wanting in hospitality, to Huguenots, Calvinists and Royalist *emigrés*. Amongst these refugees from political persecution, the Duc d'Orléans found pleasure in living in studious retirement at Twickenham. He had travelled widely, from Lapland to Sicily and from America to Switzerland, and he seemed to have a sincere regard for the English way of life. Although an exile, he refused to fight against Napoleon because it would mean taking arms against his own country, and he was gratified by the steps Castlereagh took in 1818 to bring France into an alliance of European powers. During the years that followed, this spirit of mutual understanding was often rudely shaken. In 1823 Canning wrote that the French foreign minister was 'no revolutionary scoundrel; but constitutionally hating England, and so things are getting back to a wholesome state again. Every nation for itself, and God for us all'. But the new tendency towards co-operation was not to be killed so easily, and, when in 1830 the French people, weary of rulers who had learnt nothing and forgotten nothing, gave supreme power to the Duc d'Orléans as Louis-Philippe, King of the French, an *entente* was created which lasted— uneasily sometimes, it is true—for sixteen years. As the King sought to model himself upon the English tradition, it was inevitable that he should make friendly approaches to Queen Victoria. This desire to bring two traditional enemies into better relations was strengthened in 1832, when the French king's daughter, Louise, became the second wife of Leopold, King of the Belgians, Victoria's uncle. The royal families were thus drawn closer together, and the young queen's first experience of a foreign country, and also the first visit of an English sovereign to a French one since the Field of the Cloth of Gold, was Victoria's visit to Louis's summer mansion, the Château d'Eu, near the Channel coast, in September 1843.

A year later Louis-Philippe set out from the Château d'Eu to make a return visit. It was a memorable occasion—the first on which a reigning French monarch had landed in friendship on these shores. With his son, the Duc de Montpensier, Guizot, his foreign minister, and Admiral Mackau, minister of marine, the King boarded his luxurious steam-yacht, the *Gomer*, at Tréport in the fading light of the evening of 7 October. As he set foot on deck, lights blazed from portholes, masts and rigging, while the strains of the marine band on the quay came fitfully on the breeze across the water. He looked back over the waves, now dark, now flashing with the lights of rockets, and saw a little group of flickering torches held by fisherwomen dressed in national costume. In the centre stood the Queen and his sister, the Princess Adelaide, waving farewell. The wind dropped, and the *Gomer* and her escort made the crossing swiftly and comfortably; so swiftly that she arrived before the time scheduled for her reception. A flotilla of gunboats put out to welcome the King and to escort him into harbour. The scene was one of the greatest animation; all ships were dressed and their flags flew bravely in the early breeze; the tricolour was run up in honour of the Frenchmen; the air was loud with salvo after salvo of gun-salutes, one of which was fired by Nelson's old flagship, the *Victory*, and each was answered by the French ships, while the *Gomer* steamed up and down, drawing cheers from each vessel that she passed. At last it was time for her to tie up near the Victoria Pier, and the Lords of the Admiralty went on board to greet the King. They were followed by the Mayor and Corporation of Portsmouth, who, in the state-room with its upholstery of crimson velvet and yellow satin and its fittings of rare woods, delivered speeches of welcome. After the ceremony, the King shook hands with each of the councillors, and, seeing some of them fumbling in embarrassment to remove their gloves, turned and said, 'Oh, never mind your gloves, gentlemen', a genial comment which proved all that had been reported of his dislike of the trappings of authority and which won him much popularity.

At half-past ten Prince Albert, accompanied by the Duke of Wellington, arrived by train at Gosport. They made their way at once to the harbour, amid the cheers that always greeted the public appearances of the Iron Duke. Louis-Philippe received the Prince on the deck of the *Gomer*, and the crowds on the quay received their first impression of the French king. He was still a handsome and imposing man for all his seventy-one years, and he carried his military uniform with great dignity. As soon as he greeted the Prince and the Duke, the vivacity for which he was renowned showed itself. In an atmosphere of great cordiality the royal party drove to Gosport station under arches of laurel, along streets lined with troops. As a mark of her esteem, the Queen had ordered her private railway-carriage to be placed at Louis's disposal for the journey. This carriage, recently presented to Her Majesty by the South-Western Railway for her journeys to Portsmouth and the Isle of Wight, had been furnished with unusual luxury by Herring, the upholsterer. The walls and doors were thickly quilted in white and pearl-grey damask silk, studded with crimson; the ceiling was of white watered silk, embroidered with crimson velvet and silver in relief; on the floor was a patterned Axminster carpet; the blinds were peach-coloured with silver tassels and fringes. The furniture consisted of two marble-topped tables with gilt consoles, on which stood cornucopias of flowers, and four extremely ample fixed armchairs. A second compartment, intended for the royal children, contained a sofa. Illumination was from a single overhead lamp. In an attempt to preserve the illusion of a boudoir, the windows had been made of frosted glass decorated with arabesques. The exterior of the carriage was surmounted by crowns, an elaborate cornice and a ventilator, which one of Louis's suite thought was in the shape of a pepper-pot. In this drawing-room on wheels, the royal party travelled as far as Farnborough, whence they completed the journey to Windsor in an open carriage.

Louis-Philippe drove into Windsor Castle by George IV's gateway, to the cheers of the crowd, the roar of guns, and the peal of the bells of St George's Chapel. But in contrast to this, the Queen, plainly dressed in black—for the court was still in mourning for the death of the Prince's father, the Duke of Saxe-Coburg Gotha—greeted the King with simple dignity. Louis was not alone in noticing the 'spontaneous and natural transition' by which the lively little Queen could become, on such occasions, 'the very culmination of Majesty'. The King was shown at once to his suite of rooms, which had recently been occupied by a monarch of very different convictions from his own, the Russian Tsar, Nicholas I. The rest of the day was quietly spent, in accordance with the advice Victoria had received from the Queen of the Belgians. 'My father', she had written, 'is one of the beings most easy to please, satisfy and to accommodate. His eventful life has used him to everything.' But in spite of the discipline of a hard life, in his old age he permitted himself certain small weaknesses. He must be allowed, Louise wrote, not to appear for breakfast, for eating in the morning disagreed with him; luncheon and dinner were the only meals necessary for his health. But, against this, she asked, 'Kindly order for him a bowl of chicken broth. It is the only thing he takes generally in the morning, and between

his meals.' He preferred to sleep on a horse-hair mattress laid on a plank; he should rest for two hours in the afternoon; he must not ride; and, above all, he must not be allowed to catch cold. The advice was followed, and the only excitement offered to the King that day was the presentation of the three eldest royal children, Princess Victoria, Prince Albert Edward and Princess Alice. They were led into the crowded and brightly lit reception room after dinner, and it is certain that they formed a new bond of sympathy between the old King, himself the father of eight, and the young Queen, passionately devoted to the pleasures of family life.

The next two days were also spent in leisurely fashion, viewing the royal collection of pictures and driving to places of interest in the vicinity. The trips were made in a new *char-à-bancs* which Louis-Philippe had had made for Queen Victoria in exact replica of one of his which she had admired the previous summer in France. It was painted deep blue and decorated in silver. Inside were four rows of double seats, with backs, enabling eight persons to travel in comfort. In this capacious vehicle, drawn by four white horses from the royal stables, they drove to Twickenham, where Louis had lived in exile, to Hampton Court Palace, and to Claremont House, which belonged at this time to the King of the Belgians, but where, barely six years later, on 26 August 1850, Louis-Philippe, no longer King of the French, was to die. In spite of his daughter's injunction, Louis went riding in Windsor Great Park with his hostess. These quiet, unceremonious days were most successful. The Queen liked this vivacious man who could talk so well 'upon all and every subject'. She admired 'his great activity of mind'. Even Albert thawed a little from 'his extraordinary stiffness and formality' when the King called him 'mon frère'. They both came to his rescue as they heard his comments, 'Déplorable! Pitoyable!' when he saw a speech written for him replying to the compliments of the City of London, and they collaborated with him in writing another.

In the afternoon of 11 October the climax of the visit was reached. In the throne-room of the Castle, with Prince Albert and the Duke of Cambridge as his sponsors, Louis-Philippe was created a Knight of the Order of the Garter. He was the eighth French king to enter this, one of the noblest of the orders of chivalry, and his creation was an honour which strongly appealed to the ambitious nature of a man who claimed to be a 'citizen-king' and yet possessed all the Bourbon tenaciousness of personal power. Indeed, he remarked that he had not felt that he belonged to the 'club' of European sovereigns until he had received the Order of the Garter. In the evening a banquet was held in St George's Hall, at which more than one hundred guests sat down. This was one of the occasions when the quiet, homely court

INTERIEUR DU CAROSSE DE LA REINE
A Watercolour Drawing by E. Pingret

Palais du Louvre

THE ARRIVAL OF LOUIS-PHILIPPE AT WINDSOR

A Painting by E. Pingret, at the Musée de Versailles

Musée de Versailles

transformed itself into unexpected splendour. The Tsar of Russia had been deeply impressed, and Louis-Philippe's conception of monarchy must have enabled him to appreciate the contrast between the sobriety of every-day life at Windsor and the spectacle of the great banqueting hall, crowded with guests in flashing diamonds, some in the rich robes of the Order of the Garter, others in splendid uniforms; with the long walls hung with portraits of Stuart and Hanoverian sovereigns of the Order, and with the tables gleaming with the ceremonial gold plate.

The next day a signal honour was shown to the French King, when the Lord Mayor, Aldermen and Common Council of the City of London journeyed to Windsor Castle to welcome him. This was the first time in their history that the City dignitaries had travelled beyond their boundaries for such a purpose. They were carried by train as far as Slough, where the Lord Mayor, in his robes of cloth of gold, and the Sheriffs entered their state coaches, which had been sent on before them. They made the journey to Windsor in a cavalcade of eighteen coaches, while an excited crowd gathered to watch the unique spectacle. Louis-Philippe received the company with extreme geniality, chatting informally with several whose faces were familiar to him, and replying to the addresses in the speech in excellent English which Victoria and Albert had helped him to write. This speech attracted much attention, although its authors were then unknown. During the same day, the Duc de Montpensier paid a visit to Woolwich Arsenal. On his return journey he examined and tested the newly-installed electric telegraph system operating between Paddington and Slough, the first public line to be laid. The Duke made contact with Slough and was told that the Lord Mayor of London and the Aldermen were at the station on their way back to town. They were pleased by their reception at Windsor and especially by the courteous reply made to their speeches by the Duke's father, in which he expressed in pure English his belief in the efficacy of good relations between France and England.

Meanwhile, after the mayoral party had left the Castle, Louis-Philippe paid a visit to Eton College. He had a boisterous reception, the boys' cheering being much more shrill and vigorous than monarchs are normally accustomed to receive. *The Times* recorded that 'it was with no little difficulty that such a multitude of enthusiastic and unruly madcaps could be kept in anything at all approaching to order'. But the king who kept the Palais Royal open to all who cared to come and shake hands with the head of the state was not to be perturbed by a noisy greeting. On the contrary, he seemed moved by the warmth of his welcome and favourably impressed by the school.

The last day of Louis's visit was a Sunday. There were no public functions, and the King went in the morning to hear mass at the Roman Catholic chapel at Clewer, to which he presented a fine silver gilt monstrance. The rest of the day was spent quietly in private conversation between these monarchs who understood each other so well. It is possible that the King took the opportunity to discuss the marriage of Isabella, the young Queen of Spain. She was still only a child, and it might have been supposed that the first thoughts about a suitable husband should have been left to her mother. But in Louis-Philippe's clever brain there was developing a scheme whereby the Pyrenees would be abolished. He was too subtle to make the obvious proposal that the Spanish queen should marry his son, the Duc de Montpensier, but contented himself, at first, with drawing Queen Victoria's attention to his dislike of the project that the favoured suitor should be Prince Leopold, a first cousin of Prince Albert and of the Queen herself. To Guizot, his foreign minister, he confided his plan that Isabella should marry her cousin, the Duke of Cadiz, while Montpensier married her younger sister. He had good reason to believe that the Duke of Cadiz was incapable of having children, and so, he thought, the succession would pass, in due course, to the younger sister, her husband and their children. In the atmosphere of cordiality created by Louis' visit, the subject of the Spanish marriage was opened up; it was to be closed in a very different atmosphere.

Day broke angrily on 14 October. Gusts of wind roared suddenly round the grey towers of Windsor Castle and huge clouds rolled over the green countryside. In spite of this, the arrangements for Louis-Philippe's departure were carried out. Queen Victoria, the King and the Prince, with members of the royal households, set out in six coaches from Windsor to join the train at Farnborough for Gosport. As they passed Virginia Water, four little boats on the choppy lake dressed ship and enacted a mock battle. It was not until they were comfortably settled once again in the Queen's private railway carriage and some way advanced on their journey, that the storm broke in its full force. They arrived at Gosport as premature darkness was falling. In spite of the rain and wind, an attempt was made to carry out the elaborate military honours. Troops lined the streets, salvos of guns were fired in the distance, even some of the townspeople braved the storm to watch and cheer. The music of the military bands was heard only fitfully above the rush of the wind; umbrellas blew inside out, and ladies turned their backs to the weather to prevent their skirts ballooning over their heads; the old Duke of Wellington, setting an example to his men by remaining on horseback in the storm, drew a brown great-coat over his field-marshal's uniform and buttoned it up to the chin. The small lights outlining the triumphal arches made glistening reflections in the wet streets as the Queen, the King and the Prince passed in a covered carriage. Arms were smartly presented, and the company instantly broke up.

As the royal party arrived at the harbour, they knew, by the incessant roar of the sea, that it would not be possible to adhere to the original plans for Louis' departure. The Queen and Prince Albert were to have gone on board the *Gomer*, where the King had intended to entertain them to a farewell banquet before he sailed for Tréport in the early hours of the morning. An alternative plan was hastily evolved, by which a special train was to take Louis to London, whence he would travel on by rail to Dover, crossing from there to Calais. So, after a hurried dinner and an informal farewell, the King once again boarded a train. Queen Victoria and her husband remained at Portsmouth, to spend the night on the royal yacht, fortunately lying in a sheltered part of the harbour. The next morning they were due to sail to the Isle of Wight, but, before leaving, the Queen attempted to make up for the disappointment felt by the French sailors at the abandonment of the banquet, by taking breakfast on board the *Gomer* and drinking the health of the King of the French. This set a seal on the good relations which existed during the visit. The Queen wrote a few days later to her uncle, the King of the Belgians, 'Another very great thing is, that the officers of the two Navies staying at Portsmouth were on the best terms together and paying one another every sort of compliment.' On the Friday night there had been a grand ball at the Royal Naval College, at which more than thirteen hundred people were present, for whose entertainment fifteen tons of 'refreshments and paraphernalia' were ordered. The ball was still in full swing at eight o'clock the following morning, and it is certain that the French officers carried home memories of 'every sort of compliment'.

The train took Louis-Philippe as far as Nine Elms station in London. Here a state carriage was waiting for him and he was driven, escorted by a troop of Life Guards, to New Cross. The officials of the South-Eastern Railway had had time to make only the scantiest preparations for his arrival, and even these were hindered by a sudden and disastrous outbreak of fire. The first flames were seen as workmen were hurrying to erect a canopy on the platform for Louis's departure. The police were called, but it was an hour before the fire-engines arrived from the London Fire Brigade and from Deptford dockyard. The fire originated in the paint-room in the loft of the great octagonal engine-house and was probably caused by the spontaneous ignition of some vegetable black. By the time the fire-engines arrived the flames had secured a firm hold of the inflammable paint and were being dangerously fanned by the high wind.

The harassed officials had time only to drape the waiting-room with scarlet cloth, when Louis's carriage wheeled into the station-yard at nine o'clock. Two hours later, scarcely noticed in the dark glow of flames and smoke, his special train left for Dover. The fire was still at its height—indeed, it was not until many hours after the King's departure that the flames were finally extinguished. Six engines and three tenders were destroyed in what was one of the worst fires London had known for many years.

It was two o'clock in the morning when the King eventually reached Dover. Although accustomed to the hardships of life, he must have felt that his departure from England was unduly difficult and dangerous. He spent what remained of the night at the Ship Hotel, and, when he had risen, he was formally received by the authorities of the town. The weather here, though still stormy, was quieter than it had been at Portsmouth, and the crossing to Calais was easily made in the French ship *Nord*. Louis finally reached the Château d'Eu at about ten o'clock on the evening of 15 October and was able to relieve the serious anxiety of his wife and family.

Queen Victoria was pleased with Louis's visit. On 17 October she wrote to the King of the Belgians, 'The dear King's visit went off to perfection, and I much and deeply regret its being passed. He spoke very openly to us all, and is determined that our affairs should go well.' The good impression was enhanced when the King returned to Paris and sent presents to the English royal children. But in other ways the amiability of the visit was impaired. Louis's scheme for the Spanish marriage was revealed and understood. Queen Victoria, with Prince Albert and Lord Aberdeen, paid another visit to the Château d'Eu, during which the most binding agreement was made to rule out both the claims of Prince Leopold and Louis's subtle plan for French predominance in Spain. It seemed that the danger had passed, but an indiscreet dispatch from Lord Palmerston, which fell into the hands of Guizot, gave Louis-Philippe the opportunity to think that the English were intriguing on behalf of Leopold. He immediately renewed his pressure on the Spanish Queen-Mother, and, shortly afterwards, the two marriages he had planned took place. Queen Victoria was deeply upset by what she called the French King's 'tricks and over-reachings'. She believed him to take 'a pleasure in being cleverer and more cunning than others, often when there was no advantage to be gained by it'. But his triumph was short-lived. Within eighteen months Paris rose against him and he found himself alone. He escaped with the Queen from a back entrance of the palace, and they made their way in disguise to Honfleur. There the royal couple hid in a gardener's cottage, until eventually they were smuggled out of the country by the British Consul at Le Havre and arrived at Newhaven as "Mr and Mrs Smith", 'unprovided with anything but the clothes they wore'.

THE RECEPTION OF LOUIS-PHILIPPE
A Painting by F. X. Winterhalter, at Windsor Castle

Reproduced by gracious permission of His Majesty the King

THE DEPARTURE FROM GOSPORT IN A STORM
A Lithograph after E. Pingret

In the possession of the author

THE CRYSTAL PALACE
An Engraving by G. Baxter
Guildhall Museum

The Opening of the Great Exhibition

1851

With ganial foire

Thransfuse me loyre,

Ye sacred nympths of Pindus,

The whoile I sing

That wondthrous thing,

The Palace made o' windows.

So let us raise

Victoria's praise,

And Albert's proud condition,

That takes his ayse

As he surveys

This Cristial Exhibition.

W. M. THACKERAY, Lyra Hibernica

The Opening of the Great Exhibition, 1851

I WISH YOU COULD HAVE witnessed the 1st May 1851, the greatest day in our history.' So wrote Queen Victoria to her uncle, and, allowing for the exaggeration of excitement, there was good reason for the Queen to feel that she had enjoyed a day of extraordinary achievement. The Great Exhibition, which was her husband's personal project and which had been the cause of bitter criticism, was opened that day amid scenes of triumphant enthusiasm. The Queen and her husband had walked through the exhibition, hand-in-hand with their two eldest children, enjoying all they saw in this vast shop-window of the world and giving simple pleasure to the thousands who crowded around them. And, as if it were not enough to find everything better than the wildest dreams and all the critics silenced, there had been the quiet happiness of the moment when, later in the day, the Duke of Wellington, eighty-two years old that day, had come to present a gift to his godson, Prince Arthur, on his first birthday. When Winterhalter commemorated the day, it was the domestic scene that occupied the bulk of his canvas, with the old warrior presenting a jewelled casket, and the baby offering a bunch of lilies-of-the-valley in exchange, but the triumph of the day was not forgotten; in the far corner, symbolically placed, is a distant view of the glass pavilion. This mingling of private and public satisfactions was good cause for the Queen to record that it was the happiest, proudest day in her life.

There had been many occasions in the previous two years when a successful out-come of Prince Albert's ambitious scheme had seemed most unlikely; a few moments, even, when the project was in danger of being ridiculed and criticized out of existence, with the Prince forced to carry all the censure for the blow to national prestige. But Albert was a man able not only to conceive a project but to plan its development with the minutest care and to carry it through with indefatigable perseverance. All these qualities were called into action by the arduous transactions of creating the world's first international exhibition. It was in 1849 that the Prince, his mind always devoted to science, philosophy and the arts, began to ponder how his favourite interests could be applied to the advancement of peace, progress and prosperity. In his capacity as President of the Society of Arts he sounded influential members on the possibility of holding an exhibition to show the best that every country could produce, to encourage a closer application of science and art to manufacture, powerfully to stimulate public taste, and to throw open the doors of the world to the advantages of friendly intercourse. The people he approached brought back favourable reports from manufacturers and industrialists. Five thousand of these agreed to become the promoters of the enterprise; the Colonies and the East India Company promised their support; a Royal Commission was appointed in January 1850 to give effect to the scheme—it seemed that only careful routine-work would be needed to produce the Great Exhibition in 1851.

If many of the promoters had already jumped so far ahead, the Prince, with his attention to detail, was dealing with questions of the site and the building. Through the influence of Sir Robert Peel, the government sanctioned the use of a piece of land in Hyde Park, near Rotten Row. The Building Committee received two hundred and thirty-three plans for an exhibition building, and proceeded to reject them all. The first stirrings of public criticism were heard when people began to realize that the beautiful open space of the Park, one of London's greatest amenities, was to be destroyed by a colossal building. When the building committee produced its own plan for an even vaster erection of bricks and mortar, surmounted by a mighty dome, the opposition became a storm. Newspapers and politicians led the attack, the objectives of which soon widened from the building and the site to the exhibition itself. It was said that the event would cause the country to be flooded with foreign ruffians, that there would be riots if not revolution, that honest working men would be starved by an upward rush of prices, and that the Queen would certainly be murdered. All this seriously affected the finances of the project. The Prince toiled unceasingly to build up a guarantee fund, but, at the same time, the building com-mittee clung stubbornly to their plan and so incited even more violent attacks.

In June 1850, with less than a year to go, the situation looked black. It was at this eleventh hour that a proposal was made which changed the whole outlook. Joseph Paxton, superintendent of the Duke of Devonshire's gardens at Chatsworth, had recently come into public notice by his interest in the Victoria Regia water lily. This wonderful tropical plant flowered for the first time in Europe at Chatsworth in 1849. The event was a sensation but it produced serious problems for Paxton. Twice the plant outgrew its tank, and then he designed a new type of conservatory to house the giant. Whether an enlargement of this glass-house was in Paxton's mind when he heard the criticism of the building committee's plan is not known but is is certain that one day in the middle of June, when he was presiding over a Midland Railway committee at Derby, he made the first sketch of the Crystal Palace on a sheet of blotting-paper. On 21 June, Paxton took his plans for a glass and iron structure to London and laid them before the Commissioners. Within the next few days there was intense activity. Many of the Commissioners were impressed by the novel idea of a gigantic glass-house, but time was short and the building committee were strongly entrenched behind their own plan. Paxton had two long interviews with Prince Albert, but even he, the author of the scheme, felt so uncertain that on 3 July he wrote to Baron Stockmar that the Commissioners were on the point of abandoning the exhibition altogether. Paxton was not a man to be easily thwarted. He forced the hand of the building committee by publishing his plans in the *Illustrated London News*. Public reaction was favourable; here was a means of erecting a building large enough to house the exhibition without causing permanent damage to the Park; and, although the plan had the attraction of novelty, it was not strange enough to terrify. People had only to think of the great conservatories at Kew and Chatsworth to have a picture in miniature of the proposed exhibition building. The building committee decided to give the scheme a chance, but it had still to pass the test of finance, and only a week could be allowed for the presentation of a detailed tender. Charles Dickens, writing in *Household Words*, commented on the achievement of preparing an estimate in so short a time. 'What was done in those few days? Two parties in London, relying on the accuracy and goodwill of a single ironmaster, the owners of a single glass-works in Birmingham, and of one master-carpenter in London, bound themselves for a certain sum of money and in the course of some months to cover eighteen acres of ground with a building upwards of a third of a mile long: 1851 feet (the exact date of the year), and some 450 feet broad.'

The figures were prepared at lightning speed, were delivered promptly, and proved to be acceptable both to the building committee and the Royal Commission. There was rejoicing for a day or two, and then everything had to be subordinated to the work of erecting the building in time. The contractors arrived on the site on 30 July; two months later the first column stood in position. From that moment the work proceeded at a pace that amazed the crowds which gathered every day to watch. Three thousand three hundred columns, linked by two thousand three hundred girders, and walled with four hundred tons of glass, were put up in two months. The

whole building, complete with devices for subduing the intense light and exceptional precautions to ensure its being watertight, was ready to receive the exhibits seventeen weeks after the first column was lifted into place. This speed would have been remarkable under any conditions, but it is certain that at least four weeks would have been cut from this time if Paxton's original design had not been enlarged in one important detail. When the agitation against the use of Hyde Park had been at its height, it had been pointed out that several fine elm trees were growing on the site. Paxton altered his first design, which gave the building a height of sixty-six feet, and added a transept with a semi-circular roof, one hundred and eight feet high, to enclose the trees. The glass-house was one of the first triumphs of mass production. All the elements used in its construction were of standard size and were interchangeable, not only the girders, columns, gutters and sash-bars, but the panes of glass, which were all four feet long. In this way the building was erected in a surprisingly short time, even though its designer, as some of the trade papers were quick to point out, was not an architect but only a gardener.

Although the work made such gratifying progress, all the difficulties were not yet surmounted. There were pious objections, taking the form of hints that the foreign visitors would introduce all kinds of strange immorality to corrupt the British. Prince Albert, vexed by repeated attacks, wrote to Stockmar, 'The opponents of the Exhibition work with might and main to throw all the old women into a panic, and to drive myself crazy.' But the most serious criticisms were economic and political. The supporters of protection and nationalism saw the exhibition as an attack upon the fundamentals of the English way of life. They fought back with fanatical rage. Their spokesman in the House of Commons, Colonel Sibthorp, was not content with anathematizing it as 'that fraud upon the public', he prayed for a Divine intervention to destroy it. All the narrow, fearful and selfish elements in men were appealed to; but all the appeals were met by the firm, sensible, broad-minded outlook of the Prince. He had wished to remain in the background and let the Commissioners carry out the project, but, when the storms broke, he was the only one sufficiently convinced of the worthiness of the scheme to be able to proceed with confidence. Fortunately, he soon won staunch supporters. *The Times*, at first antagonistic, came to his aid; the *Illustrated London News*, proud of its place in the scheme as the first publisher of Paxton's original design, continued to illustrate the progress of the work week by week and so enabled people all over the country to appreciate the work of transformation which was taking place in Hyde Park; and, perhaps most important of all, *Punch* threw in the cheerful good humour of its support. As early as August 1850 the humorists of Bouverie Street

1851: THE FIRST OF MAY
A Painting by F. X. Winterhalter at Windsor Castle

Reproduced by gracious permission of His Majesty the King

THE GRAND ENTRANCE TO THE GREAT EXHIBITION
An Engraving by G. Baxter

Victoria and Albert Museum

drew attention to Paxton's gifts by suggesting that he should design for the Lords and Commons two 'Houses of Glass', complete with a pane of magnifying power here and there 'to make any favourite Minister look a greater man than he is'. This was a critical comment on Barry, the architect, whose Houses of Parliament had then been ten years building, but not even the mockery of *Punch* could hasten that ponderous undertaking. It was to be another eighteen years before the Palace of Westminster was complete. Meanwhile Paxton worked in terms of weeks not years, and the speed with which he fulfilled his undertakings won him increased support. The most valuable stroke on his behalf was Douglas Jerrold's happy inspiration in coining the nickname, 'the Crystal Palace'. In spite of Ruskin's comment that 'it is neither a palace nor of crystal', from the moment of its christening in *Punch* to the time of the destruction of the altered building at Sydenham, it carried for millions of people the happiest associations of a palace of pleasure.

As the work on the building proceeded, Prince Albert immersed himself in world-wide correspondence to obtain the co-operation of other countries. He encountered great difficulties, but they were overcome, and early in 1851 he began to feel confident that the building would be ready, that there would be fifteen thousand exhibitors, more than half of them from forty foreign nations, and that their goods, divided into four classes of raw materials, machinery, manufactures and fine arts, would be displayed in ten miles of stands, decorated by Owen Jones with a splendour reminiscent of the courts of the Alhambra. Then a further problem arose, so ridiculous that it seemed the last straw brought into existence specifically to break the camel's back. A grave danger to the rich exhibits from East and West was threatened by the presence inside the building of a flock of sparrows inhabiting the elm trees. The Commissioners, worn out by greater worries, were defeated by this small one. The Duke of Wellington, as Ranger of Hyde Park, was consulted by the Queen. His advice, terse and pointed, was typical of a great soldier: 'Try sparrow-hawks, ma'am'. The sparrows were defeated, except a few which were seen by Berlioz when he visited the exhibition, and surreptitiously fed by him. Early on the morning of 1 May 1851 the great International Exhibition was ready to open its doors to the public—at least, almost ready. At the last moment, Lord Granville, one of the Commissioners, was busy sweeping up some dust before the Royal dais.

It was a cloudy morning as thousands of people, all bustle and excitement, gathered to watch the Queen drive from Buckingham Palace to Hyde Park. At half-past eleven the whole procession of state carriages was in motion. It was a day of pleasure; the Queen found everyone 'in the highest good humour' and contributed herself to the atmosphere by riding not in a state coach but in one of the carriages she used for visits to the theatre. A little rain fell as they left the Palace, but, as they came in sight of the Park, the sun broke through the clouds and 'gleamed upon the gigantic edifice, upon which the flags of all the Nations were floating'. The Queen recorded, 'The Green Park and Hyde Park were one densely crowded mass of human beings', but there were no accidents and no incidents. The riots and revolution failed to occur; even more distressing for the prophets of doom, people were enjoying themselves. Charles Greville looked at the crowds with wonder: 'no soldiers, hardly a policeman to be seen.' The carriages drove up Rotten Row; the Queen descended and entered the Crystal Palace as the flourish of trumpets echoed and re-echoed in the lofty aisles.

Prince Albert led the Queen and their two eldest children, the Princess Royal and the Prince of Wales, to the central transept, where, in a carefully chosen position between the famous elm trees and the crystal fountain, one of the features of the exhibition, a dais had been erected. It was covered with a magnificent carpet specially woven for the occasion by one hundred and fifty ladies. The sight of the Royal Family walking hand-in-hand towards the chair of state brought a spontaneous roar of enthusiasm from the great crowds filling the galleries and courts. The Queen was beautifully dressed in pink watered silk, brocaded with silver and diamonds, but it was not robes alone that gave her such an air of majesty as she stood by the chair ('which I did *not* sit on,' she recorded). Perhaps it was because she felt proud of her husband and her country, while thousands of voices sang 'God Save the Queen'.

Prince Albert then left the dais and stood at the head of the Commissioners—'a curious assemblage', thought the Queen. He read a long report of the aims of the exhibition, to which Victoria read a short answer. The Archbishop of Canterbury offered up a prayer, and then the choir of six hundred voices, with the organ and two hundred instruments, burst into the 'Hallelujah Chorus'. The Queen said it 'sounded like nothing', because of the immensity of the building. At this moment a Chinese mandarin stepped forward and made his obeisance. The Queen was impressed and specially recorded the event. It was rumoured afterwards that the man was an impostor, but he did not seem out-of-place in this fancy-dress parade of the nations and added a touch of oriental dignity to the procession of diplomatic representatives, which followed the Queen on a grand tour of inspection.

The unostentatious nature of this royal procession gave immense pleasure to the crowds of visitors. It had been suggested that the exhibition should be opened at eleven o'clock for the season ticket-holders only, but the Queen and her Prime Minister would have none of this. The public should be admitted, the Queen and her family would walk amongst them and they would all enjoy the great day together. Two gentlemen were in attendance to request the visitors not to crowd around the Queen, and the nave was to be kept free of people while the royal procession passed through. The two gentlemen seem to have found the crowds too much for their polite requests; the Queen recorded, 'The nave was full, which had not been intended; but still there was no difficulty, and the whole long walk from one end to the other was made in the midst of continued and deafening cheers and waving of handkerchiefs.' The royal party returned to the dais, and Prince Albert requested Lord Breadalbane to declare that the exhibition was opened. 'Her Majesty commands me to declare this Exhibition open.' The loud voice rang through the nave, a fanfare of trumpets sounded, there was an immense cheer, in the distance a royal salute was fired, and the Great Exhibition was open, not only to the thirty thousand people who flocked there that day, but to the six million who visited it during the next five and a half months.

At home the Queen wrote excitedly in her diary and her correspondence about 'a day which makes my heart swell with pride and glory and thankfulness'. She did not forget the one to whose inventive talent so much was owed. 'All the Commissioners seemed truly happy, and no one more so than Paxton, who may be justly proud; he rose from being a common gardener's boy.' But most of her thoughts were for her husband in his immense triumph. Two days later she wrote to her uncle, the King of the Belgians, 'Albert's dearest name is immortalized with this great conception, his own, and my own dear country showed she was worthy of it.' To Lord John Russell she wrote of the Prince's 'very extraordinary powers of mind and heart'. She said she felt so proud of being his wife that she could not refrain from herself paying a tribute to his noble character. The Prince, worn out with over-work and sleeplessness, his real feelings always concealed behind a mask of formality, said only that the result of his efforts was 'quite satisfactory'.

The Crystal Palace, as an achievement, was greeted with public favour as strong as the criticism it had endured while it was a project. It was a glorious popular entertainment at a time when the round of pleasure was severely limited. Even twenty years later the plaint was raised that, with the exception of the Crystal Palace, there was not 'a single spot in London where respectable people may seek amusement out of doors without their sense of decency being outraged'. The Queen, remembering that 'a certain set of fashionables', had tried to ruin her husband's scheme, now set a popular fashion which ran far and wide amongst all her people. With her family, she visited the exhibition almost every day, even on the shilling days. The Duke of Devonshire was gazing at a colossal amazon in bronze on horseback when a small woman accosted him. 'Ma'am? said I—and—ecco! it was the Queen.' Vast crowds came to see the strange and beautiful things from many countries, with the exciting foreigners who had brought them; to admire, with feelings of patriotic pride, the results of British industry and craftsmanship; to consume hundreds of thousands of buns and bottles of lemonade— the exhibition was strictly teetotal; but, especially, to see the Queen enjoying herself.

One of the seals of success on the Great Exhibition was the fact that it closed before the public tired of it. When the doors shut on Saturday, 11 October, there was universal regret, and when the Queen paid her farewell visit in private three days later, she found it still looking 'so beautiful', As the organ played, she moved round the great building, amongst the workmen removing the glass fountain and the exhibits, and thought how sad and strange it was that 'this great and bright time has passed away like a dream, after all its triumph and success'. While the Queen and her subjects lamented the closing of the pleasure palace, it is possible that Prince Albert debated with himself whether the original objects had been achieved. If he was too close to the event to be able to answer such questions, many critics in the following years were quick to record that, in a time of great industrial expansion, the exhibition was not needed as a stimulus to British industry; that its influence on public taste was deplorable; and that while it brought people of many nations together for the first time, it taught them nothing of the wisdom of understanding. Some even went as far as to suggest that the Commissioners would have done better to have made an exhibition of the way the poor were housed and to have hidden their heads in shame. But such 'cui bono men', as Scott described them, took a limited view. They looked back to the simple elegance of taste in the early eighteenth century and saw only the riot of meaningless ornament housed at the Crystal Palace; they thought of Queen Victoria's enthusiasm for the 'Peace Festival' and remembered that within three years Britain had plunged herself into the Crimean War. But there were at least two real justifications of the Great Exhibition. The first was the purpose on which the large profit was spent—the provision of a 'locality' in South Kensington to contain a group of buildings for the development of industrial education. To this far-sighted enterprise is due the Victoria and Albert Museum, the Natural History Museum, the Imperial College of Science, the Albert Hall, the Royal College of Music, and other buildings which form the most important group of cultural institutions in London. The other, imponderable but far-reaching in its consequences, was that millions of people, pausing for a moment in the midst of drab, restricted, workaday lives, enjoyed themselves.

THE OPENING OF THE GREAT EXHIBITION

A Watercolour Drawing by J. Nash at Windsor Castle

Reproduced by gracious permission of His Majesty the King

THE GREAT EXHIBITION FROM THE SERPENTINE
A Watercolour Drawing by William Wyld at Windsor Castle
Reproduced by gracious permission of His Majesty the King

The Wedding of the Prince of Wales and Princess Alexandra

1863

Sea-kings' daughter from over the sea,
Alexandra!
Saxon and Norman and Dane are we,
But all of us Danes in our welcome of thee,
Alexandra!

TENNYSON, A Welcome to Alexandra

H.R.H. THE PRINCESS ALEXANDRA CAROLINE
OF DENMARK IN HER WEDDING DRESS
H.R.H. ALBERT EDWARD, PRINCE OF WALES
Lithographs by Day, after Robert Dudley
In the possession of the author

The Wedding of the Prince of Wales and Princess Alexandra, 1863

ON A SPRING DAY in 1590 forty-two young men, dressed in white taffeta, hung with gold chains, and wearing black visors on their faces, danced before Anne of Denmark all the way from the West Port of Edinburgh to the Palace of Holyroodhouse. It was not only a happy introduction of the Danish princess to her capital city but the first record of many gay celebrations of marriages linking the royal families of Britain and Denmark. In 1683 the Princess Anne, daughter of James II, later to rule as Queen Anne, married Prince George of Denmark. They loved a life of retirement, but the King showed his new son-in-law at least one vivid example of English pageantry when he installed him as a Knight of the Garter at Windsor in 1684. Sixty years later the Crown Prince Frederick of Denmark married the Princess Louisa, the youngest daughter of George II, and then it was Copenhagen which displayed, in processions, fireworks and music, the happiness of the two nations. In a little more than twenty years there were more celebrations when Christian VII of Denmark married the Princess Carolina Matilda, daughter of the Prince of Wales. The wedding took place at Copenhagen but the festivities were continued in 1768 in London, when the Danish king visited this country. Nicknamed by Horace Walpole 'the Puppet of the day', he passed from one great house to another, in a whirl of gaiety, culminating in the superb masquerade he gave at the Haymarket. Nearly a century passed before the news of another Anglo-Danish marriage gave pleasure in both countries. On 25 November 1862 *The Times* announced the betrothal of Albert Edward, Prince of Wales, and the Princess Alexandra, elder daughter of Prince Christian of Denmark.

The Prince of Wales was twenty-one when the announcement of his engagement was made public. His recent life had been clouded by the sudden death of his father, Prince Albert, in the previous December, and the violence of his mother's grief. It was considered wise for him to adhere to plans formed by his father and to make a tour in the Holy Land in the spring of 1862. He thus extended the field of his travel which already included many European countries, Canada and the United States. His father's belief in the educative power of foreign travel was one of the more agreeable features of the strict discipline under which he was brought up. Opportunities to indulge this pleasantly became more frequent after the marriage of his sister

to the Crown Prince of Prussia. The young Prince was good-humoured and gentle, but he did not take easily to serious study. Metternich said that he looked '*très triste*', but that was perhaps not surprising as he had just received a solemn memorandum from the Queen and Prince Albert, commencing 'Life is composed of duties'. It was a pleasure to escape from the carefully-planned studies and the overpowering solicitude, to visit the Emperor in Paris, the Pope, or King Pedro at Lisbon. But pleasure became carefree when he could go to Potsdam and stay with his clever and sympathetic sister. On these journeys he acquired that fluent command of foreign languages which helped him in later years to continue his father's work as 'a promoter of international friendliness'. What was even more remarkable was that, at so early an age and while still under the influence of a rather repressive upbringing, it could be said of him, on his trips abroad, that he 'was popular with those who do not easily learn to like either Englishmen or Princes'.

Ten years before the engagement, events had occurred which had radically altered the fortunes of Princess Alexandra's family. Her father and mother, Prince Christian of Schleswig-Holstein and Princess Louise of Hesse, were both closely related to Frederick VII, King of Denmark, but, as they were not in the direct line of succession, they lived quietly at the Castle of Bernsdorf, near Copenhagen. Here, in country surroundings far removed from the splendours of the court, the Princess spent her childhood. In 1852, as Frederick was childless, it became essential to make provision for the succession to the Danish throne. Representatives of the great powers met in London and selected Prince Christian to succeed to the crown on the death of the reigning king. By a stroke of the pen the position of Christian and his family was completely changed. From being a prince of little importance, he became the heir to the throne, while his wife, who had family relationships with nearly all the European sovereigns, came to be called 'the aunt of all Europe'. The family moved to the Amalienborg Palace in Copenhagen. Princess Alexandra was eight years old when these changes occurred, but her life remained marked by an engaging simplicity.

In September 1862, the Prince of Wales travelled to Germany to watch the autumn manœuvres of the Prussian army at Breughl. It is possible that the visit had another purpose. After a few days he left and joined his sister at Coblenz. Together they travelled up the Rhine, until on 24 September they came to Speier. There, in the magnificent Romanesque cathedral, he saw Princess Alexandra for the first time. She was travelling with her family on one of the journeys through Germany that they frequently made. The two royal parties joined for a trip to Heidelberg, where they stayed three days. It is recorded of the Prince and Princess that 'each made a good impression on the other'. The Prince of Wales returned to his studies at Cambridge, from which he was summoned by his father's sudden death in December. Many months elapsed before Edward and Alexandra were able to meet again—months during which the Prince not only saw the Holy Land but was entertained by the Sultan at Constantinople and the King of Greece at Athens. In August of that year, Prince Christian and his family were holiday-making at Ostend, when Queen Victoria decided to stay for a few days at Brussels on her way to Germany. Her uncle and host, the King of the Belgians, invited the Danish family to meet her. This was the first time that Queen Victoria had seen the young Princess, and, from her first impressions, she provided one of the earliest descriptions of a lady who remained renowned for her beauty for more than sixty years. She 'looked lovely, in a black dress, nothing in her hair, and curls on either side, which hung over her shoulders, her hair turned back off her beautiful forehead. Her whole appearance was one of the greatest charm, combined with simplicity and perfect dignity'. The Queen resumed her journey, and immediately the Prince of Wales arrived in Belgium from England. There was a happy party at the Palace at Laeken. On 9 September the Prince and Princess spent a considerable time together in the garden, and that evening, at dinner, King Leopold proposed the health of their Royal Highnesses as affianced bride and bridegroom.

If Queen Victoria never ceased to treat her eldest son as a child, she yet understood her own people. Writing to Lord John Russell, she emphasized the importance of the marriage 'being in no sense considered a political one', while to the King of the Belgians she revealed her mind even more clearly: 'The match is really quite a love match; Bertie is extremely happy and in admiration of his very lovely bride. All the arguments that one forced him to marry a young lady he had never seen, fall most completely to the ground; and this is important, particularly for England, where it will please people very much that the Prince of Wales, like his parents, should marry from affection.' In November, while the Prince was in Italy, Queen Victoria invited the Princess and her father to stay at Windsor. The visit was private, but rumour was already painting a charming picture of the Princess who might become the future Queen. Before the Danish royal party left the Castle the formal announcement had

been made. In the shower of congratulations that followed, the Prince, on his way home, rushed from Paris to meet his bride at Lille. Together they travelled to the Danish border.

The Queen gave her consent for the wedding to take place in March. At first it seemed that, because of the gloomy seclusion in which the Queen now lived, the event would be robbed of much of its pageantry. The City of London recorded its respectful but sincere feeling of disappointment at the announcements that there would be no outward manifestations of rejoicing on the occasion of the Princess's arrival and that the wedding would be held at the Chapel Royal, Windsor. It was then announced that a state reception would be held but that the scene of the wedding would not be transferred to Westminster Abbey or St Paul's Cathedral. A further sense of disappointment that there would be no royal functions in London before the wedding was overcome when the Prince of Wales held a levée for his mother at St James's Palace, thus obtaining his first experience of a ceremonial occasion. Meanwhile, residences were provided for the Prince and Princess. The estate of Sandringham was purchased out of the income accumulated during his minority, and Marlborough House, to become virtually the centre of the court during the Queen's retirement from London, was provided at public expense.

On 26 February Princess Alexandra commenced her journey to London. A route was chosen which would take her as much as possible through territories ruled by her own or her future husband's relations, thus ensuring a progress that combined public magnificence and family rejoicing. On a mild and sunny afternoon she drove through the streets of Copenhagen to the railway station. The people, holding their gentle and beautiful princess in special affection, crowded the streets with arms full of the earliest spring flowers, which they threw into the carriage. Across the darkening countryside the royal train carried Alexandra and her parents to the port of Korsör, where the royal yacht, *Schleswig*, was waiting to receive them. As they arrived, the ships in the harbour were brilliantly illuminated, and the night sky, now stormy with high winds, was lit with the coloured glitter of fireworks. Early the next morning the yacht sailed for Kiel, but the young princess, distressed at parting from her home and suffering from a cold, did not appear on deck until the afternoon. In a short time the great harbour of Kiel came into view and the town, then still in Danish possession, rang with the sound of welcoming bells. The Princess was greeted by her uncle, Prince Charles of Schleswig-Holstein, who conducted her to his palace. As she mounted the steps she was greeted by eighty ladies of the district, all dressed in red and white. There was a sumptuous banquet and, in the early evening, the royal

PRINCESS ALEXANDRA ARRIVING AT THE BRICKLAYERS ARMS STATION
A Lithograph by Day, after Robert Dudley

In the possession of the author

A VISIT TO ETON SCHOOL

A Lithograph by Day, after Robert Dudley

In the possession of the author

party left by train for Altona. Here the Princess received the last farewells of her own people, before driving, with an escort of dragoons, into the Hanseatic city of Hamburg. Lights shone from every window, braziers flamed in the streets, and illuminations were reflected in the waters of the Alster, as the Princess was conveyed to the Hotel de l'Europe.

The next morning the royal party, growing larger at each halt, drove to Harburg and took train for Hanover. Now commenced the portion of the journey that lay through the independent German states. The rulers vied with each other in honouring the Princess, providing a series of receptions that seemed a farewell to their own greatness, so soon to be submerged in the German empire, under the domination of Prussia. At Hanover, the state carriages of the King, a cousin of Queen Victoria, were waiting to take her to the Palace of Herrenhausen, where a family banquet of great magnificence had been prepared. The following day, 1 March, was a Sunday, and the Princess attended Divine Service conducted by the King's English chaplain, before leaving by special train for Cologne. *En route*, there were two brief stops, the first at Bucheburg, where the Prince and Princess of Lippe offered her refreshments, and the other at Minden, where Prince Albert welcomed her to Prussian territory. It was nine o'clock at night when the train arrived at Deutz, opposite Cologne, but the station was crowded with spectators to see the Princess greeted by the Duke of Nassau. On Monday the royal party passed into Belgium, where there was not only an official reception at Liége but spontaneous outbursts of rejoicing at every station on the line. At Brussels there were banquets at the palace, a command performance at the theatre, and a visit to Laeken, a palace which held happy memories for Alexandra. The King of the Belgians, now an old man but still the dominant figure amongst the European monarchs, spared nothing to give a brilliant farewell to the Princess. Her marriage was to be the last of the dynastic unions that he had planned and contrived for over thirty years. Worn out by his discreet and fatherly guidance, not only of his own country but of a great part of Europe, he died in 1865.

On 5 March Princess Alexandra started on the last stage of her journey to England. She went by train to Antwerp, where the royal yacht, *Victoria and Albert*, was waiting to convey her to the Thames. The Channel Fleet, consisting of Britain's newest ironclads, did not attempt the passage of the Scheldt, but remained off Flushing, to guard the yacht during the crossing. As the Queen's yacht came to the mouth of the river, the batteries at Flushing fired a salute, and the Princess saw for the first time the impressive sight of a British fleet with yards manned. She remarked that there was no cheering, but that every man held his hat aloft with outstretched arm. As the favour-

able weather seemed unlikely to last, it was decided to cross that night, instead of remaining at anchor off Flushing, as had been planned. The sea was smooth as glass and the Princess was walking on deck in the quiet darkness when she saw another sign of the great welcome that awaited her. Ships of the fleet lighted up all their ports, burned blue lights at the yard-arms, and displayed the cipher 'A' in bright lanterns rigged out over the stern. As the royal yacht passed through these glittering lights and their reflections in the dark sea, the ships took up their positions and closed the rear of this great water pageant. So they crossed the channel and anchored in Margate Roads at eleven o'clock at night.

On Friday, 6 March, after the Princess had been welcomed by the people of Margate, the royal squadron sailed in the evening for the Nore. The weather was stormy, but as the yacht steamed slowly out of the darkness, the glare of bonfires and fireworks greeted her from the shore, the white ensign was dipped all along the line of the assembled fleet, and the Dannebrog was hoisted. The *Victoria and Albert* anchored for the night, and the next morning ran smoothly up to Gravesend. There was excitement in the riverside town when the Prince of Wales, gaily dressed in a bright blue frock-coat, went down the gangway from the pier and boarded the royal yacht—excitement which grew when the bride and bridegroom landed together, drove through the streets in an open carriage and finally left Gravesend in a special railway carriage decorated in rosewood and white satin, drawn by an engine disguised with garlands of flowers. The Queen, in seclusion at Windsor, recorded that there was 'bustle and agitation everywhere. The preparations in London and all over the country quite wonderful, and people are very anxious it should be known that it is meant out of love and affection to us both'. The preparations were certainly elaborate. Bricklayers' Arms Station had been converted into a gigantic conservatory, the roof entirely concealed by thousands of red and white roses hanging in patterns against a background of evergreens. Lunch was served in a saloon specially decorated with walnut furniture, covered with geranium-coloured silk, and maroon and gold hangings. When the procession formed outside the station and drove through Southwark towards the city, there were frequent delays as the crowds broke through the lines of troops and swarmed round the carriages. On every building flags fluttered, at every corner stood triumphal arches, allegorical paintings, pedestals supporting armed Danes, masts bearing the Danish elephant and tower, in a riot of colours and profusion of styles that could only have existed in England after the Great Exhibition. Near the Mansion House the crowd was so vast that the procession was completely broken; even the troopers of the Life Guards were unable to move for the people who were pressed against their horses. As the royal carriage swayed perilously in the crush, the Princess instinctively stretched out her hand in alarm and found it shaken by an enthusiastic well-wisher. At last, a way through the crowd was made, and the procession moved slowly past St Paul's, Temple Bar, along the Strand, Pall Mall, Piccadilly, Hyde Park, and so to Paddington Station. Hours late, the Princess, exhausted but still smiling, realizing to the full the turbulent excitement of London's welcome, came to Slough station and was driven in darkness and pouring rain through the illuminated arches at Eton and Windsor to the castle above the river. There, on the grand staircase, the lonely Queen was waiting to greet her.

During the next two days visitors flocked into Windsor to be ready for the wedding on Tuesday, 10 March. The hotels were unable to accommodate the crowds, who overflowed into lodgings anywhere near the town. Of all the preparations the one that aroused the greatest interest was the immense Gothic hall which had been specially built at the west end of St George's Chapel. This contained robing and dressing-rooms and a hall for the marshalling of the procession. The Princess's boudoir was hung with Nottingham lace. There were rumours of the incredible jewels to be worn by the Maharajah Duleep Singh and the even more wonderful necklace of over two thousand diamonds, a wedding gift from the King of Denmark to the young princess. People told each other of the protests of High Churchmen because the wedding was to take place in Lent, and how the Queen had replied, 'In my young days, there was no Lent.' At sunrise the royal standard was flying over the castle, and at eight o'clock the bells of Windsor commenced the wedding peal. But much earlier than this the streets were packed with a solid mass of people, most of whom would see nothing but were content to stand and listen.

The Queen herself left a record of her own feelings on this memorable day: 'Cold from nervousness and agitation, I dressed, wearing my weeds, but a silk gown with *crêpe*, a long veil to my cap, and, for the first time since December '61, the ribbon, star, and badge of the Order of the Garter.' At half-past eleven the Queen went privately from the castle and took her place in Catharine of Aragon's oak closet in St George's Chapel. Although she could be seen only with difficulty, everyone in the Chapel rose and turned towards the closet. 'When I stepped up to the window,' wrote the Queen, 'the Chapel full of smartly dressed people, the Knights of the Garter in their robes, the waving banners, the beautiful window, altar, and reredos to my beloved one's memory, with the bells ringing outside, quite had the effect of a scene in a play.' Below her in the Chapel, amongst the smartly dressed people, old Lord Palmerston had just finished tidying his whiskers with a comb, and the beautiful

Countess Spencer, in a dark cerulean gown covered with lace belonging to Marie Antoinette, was attracting admiring glances. The procession of the royal guests was delayed because little Prince Waldemar of Denmark begged not to go to church but to be allowed to stay in a corridor of the castle and play with a new donkey he had been given, and when his mother still urged it, he said he had a bad cold.

At twelve o'clock the trumpeters sounded a fanfare and the drummers beat a roll, to herald the procession of the royal family. Mary Stanley recorded that 'the Queen was agitated and restless. At the first blast of the trumpets, she quivered all over and you could see the working of her face'. Everyone agreed that the entry of the English princesses was far the most beautiful of the processions, Princess Mary of Cambridge leading the way and the Queen's five daughters ending it. 'There was a pause,' wrote the Queen, 'and then the trumpets sounded again, and our boy, supported by Ernest (Coburg) and Fritz (the Crown Prince of Prussia), all in Garter robes, entered; Bertie looked pale and nervous. He bowed to me, and during the long wait for his Bride kept constantly looking up at me, with an anxious, clinging look, which touched me much. At length she appeared, the band playing Handel's *Processional March*, with her eight Bridesmaids, looking very lovely. She was trembling and very pale. Dearest Albert's *Chorale* was sung, which affected me much, and then the service proceeded. When it was over, the young couple looked up at me, and I gave them an affectionate nod and kissed my hand to sweet Alix.' The guns fired as the ring was put on and again at the end of the ceremony.

Lunch was served in the dining-room to the royal family and in St George's Hall to all the other royal guests, but the Queen lunched alone. Afterwards, something of the confusion that occurred at the state entry into London happened again at Windsor. The crowds were so thick in the streets that the great ones of the land had difficulty in getting to the station. The Archbishop of Canterbury set out to walk from the castle and found himself helpless in the centre of the crowd. He saw a policeman and cried out, 'Policeman, what can I do?' 'Hold on to the next carriage, your Grace,' was the reply, 'it's your only chance.' So as the next carriage struggled through the crowd, he seized the rear portion and there found, also hanging on, Lady Cranworth and Mr Thackeray. 'Oh,' said Lady Cranworth, 'I am so glad to see you, my Lord. I felt so ashamed of my place. Now I am satisfied.'

In the castle the Queen was still writing. 'All is over and this (to me) most trying day is past, as a dream. Bertie has taken his lovely, pure, sweet Bride to Osborne, such a jewel whom he is indeed lucky to have obtained. Here I sit lonely and desolate.'

THE BRIDESMAIDS

A Lithograph by Day, after Robert Dudley

In the possession of the author

THE SIGNING OF THE MARRIAGE ATTESTATION

A Lithograph by Day, after Robert Dudley

In the possession of the author

Norman Hartnell.

THE DESIGN FOR
PRINCESS ELIZABETH'S
WEDDING DRESS
A Sketch by Norman Hartnell
Reproduced by courtesy of Norman Hartnell, Esq.

The Wedding of Princess Elizabeth and Prince Philip, the Duke of Edinburgh

1947

Ceremonies are the outward
expression of inward feeling.

LAO-TZE

The Wedding of Princess Elizabeth and Prince Philip, the Duke of Edinburgh, 1947

SPLENDOUR HAS ALWAYS ABOUT IT, even at the moment of greatest rejoicing, a faint air of melancholy. Nothing is a sharper symbol of celebration than the glitter of fireworks in the night sky—but what of the moment when they drop in a fading curve to the still water below? The occasions of festival pass so swiftly; always they call up memories of the past, tempting us to travel back along a triumphal way crowded with pageantry which grows brighter as it recedes. When the English ships sailed with rejoicing to Scheveningen to bring back Charles Stuart to his throne, there may have been those who remembered what they had heard of the great cavalcade of one hundred and thirty horsemen, all in black vizards, who had ridden by torch-light over London Bridge three centuries before, to pay homage to the new King Richard at his palace at Kennington. When Princess Alexandra landed at Gravesend there were some who thought of the young men dressed in white taffeta, who danced before another Danish princess through the streets of Edinburgh. Talleyrand spoke for more than himself or his own countrymen when he said that those who had not known the last ten years of the *ancien régime* had never tasted the joy of living. In all countries and at all times there have been those who see the brightness of the world always ten years away and around them nothing but the French Revolution. If this sense of the past enchanted those of other ages, with what deadly fascination will it lure those who look across the devastation of two world wars. 'One cannot laugh for ever,' said Carlo Gozzi, and many now believe that if the days of laughter were limited in Gozzi's Venice they have been finally terminated in Belsen and Hiroshima. We look backwards and see gaiety dancing a long way off; we look around us and see—a young princess riding with all the panoply of ancient state through the streets of London. The streets were grey with November weather and dusty memories, but were full of people. With a flash of scarlet and blue, a gleam of steel, and a sweep of white plumes, the Household Cavalry rode down Constitution Hill, a sight most of the onlookers had thought they would never see again.

It was against a background not only of the aftermath of war but of a twilight in which the beauty and happiness of the world seemed lost that the announcement was made which, eighteen weeks later, brought the people into the streets. 'It is with the greatest pleasure that the King and Queen announce the betrothal of their dearly beloved daughter The Princess Elizabeth to Lieutenant Philip Mountbatten, R.N., son of the late Prince Andrew of Greece and Princess Andrew (Princess Alice of Battenberg), to which union the King has gladly given his consent.' At first the prospect of festivity made no impression in a world from which splendour had been absent so long. It seemed that the tradition had been broken; seven centuries of recorded grandeur, and behind them a long line of Norman and Saxon ceremonials. In Italy, where public rejoicing is more clearly demonstrated, it could be said, 'The word festivity, that magic word, is never uttered without rapture.' It was never so in England, and in 1947 we had not emerged from the dark places of a world at war. The spirit that had survived the ordeal was heard in the question whether public money should be put to such wasteful use, but slowly that other spirit, of equal antiquity, that knows that after the battle there is rejoicing, reasserted itself. The people who had welcomed the wedding of a former Princess Elizabeth with celebrations extending over months and had greeted Princess Alexandra with a reception so tumultuous that the procession could not make its way through the cheering crowds, remembered how to honour the wedding of the Heir Presumptive.

The quiet grace of an autumnal wedding matched the mood of people only just emerging from eight years of unpromising life. The preparations were soberly made, the announcements that the wedding would take place on Thursday, 20 November; that the honeymoon would be spent at Broadlands and at Birkhall; that the Princess and her husband would live at Clarence House, formerly the residence of the Duke of Connaught; and, after some hesitation and a little less soberly, that the escort of Household Cavalry would be restored to the splendour of their full-dress uniform. It was a temptation to slip down perfumed avenues of the past, to watch the young women of London scattering golden leaves and hear them crying 'Flower of the World', as Henry V rode by, glittering from his victory at Agincourt, or to loiter by the green canals as Queen Henrietta Maria was conveyed into the city of Amsterdam in a barge drawn by living swans. But the sedate preparations continued in a world of a very different colour. Gifts, costly and rare, simple and useful, arrived in profusion,

from kings and governments, schoolgirls and factory workers. Occasionally there were hints of the ancient magic. The government of Burma sent a necklace of ninety-six pigeon-blood rubies, each stone a charm against the ninety-six diseases which, according to Burmese lore, afflict humanity. On Monday, 17 November, at a dinner party given by the King and Queen at Buckingham Palace for their royal visitors, the Princess wore the ribbon of the Order of the Garter for the first time, and the next day Prince Philip was created Duke of Edinburgh, Earl of Merioneth, Baron Greenwich, and a Knight Commander of the Order of the Garter. That night, the State Apartments at Buckingham Palace, silent for eight years, resounded to the gaiety of twelve hundred guests.

Thursday, 20 November was grey and mild. There was rain in the early morning, but thousands of people stood in the streets and followed with eager delight the details of the pageantry, unspectacular, perhaps, when judged by the records of the past, but bright with promise when seen as the first carefree writing on the margin of our darkened history. The Queen and Princess Margaret, in the glass coach, leading a procession of royal guests; the Duke of Edinburgh driving swiftly past the Palace a few moments before his bride was due to leave; the National Anthem played by the Scots Guards in the Palace quadrangle as the King and Princess Elizabeth drove along the Mall in the Irish state coach, with a Sovereign's escort of the Household Cavalry; the occasional gleams of sunshine as this procession, with its richly charged memories of magnificence, swept through the cheering crowds; and the sharp beating of the drums of the Grenadier Guards as the bride alighted at Westminster Abbey.

Within the Abbey the beautiful ceremony followed its traditional course, enclosed within two silver streams of music, the trumpet fanfares with which the procession of the bride was announced and with which the signing of the register was celebrated. 'It is music,' said Havelock Ellis, 'that moulds the manners and customs that are comprised under ceremony.' The grave movements of the participants; the solemn procession of the banners of the Abbey; the moment, memorable to all who saw it, when the bride and bridegroom paused before Queen Mary and made reverence

PRINCESS ELIZABETH
AND THE DUKE OF EDINBURGH
A Photograph by Baron

THE SCENE INSIDE THE ABBEY

London Electrotype Agency

with curtsey and deep bow. They passed from the thundering music of the organ to the clamour of the bells outside and drove together in the glass coach through cheering people, who by this event, had renewed contact with that splendour which not only glorifies the sense of the past but brings to the view of the future a confidence and a pleasure too long absent from our lives.

Late that afternoon, the Princess and her husband drove to Waterloo Station on the first stage of their honeymoon journey. As the train glided out, its lights flashed on the steel and plumes and colours of the travelling escort of the Household Cavalry drawn up in line alongside the platform—a last glimpse of the grandeur of the day, made even more beautiful by the autumn dusk and the alternating light and shadow of the station. As the train disappeared down the line and the troopers turned to ride away, thoughts may have risen in the minds of even the most critical of the spectators; that this panoplied splendour is no mere anachronism. It is, rather, a symbol by which people may enter into the truth of their history. They may not completely understand it; they probably cannot explain it. But they know that it is precious to them; it is a light shining through a dark wood.

That this quality should fade from English life is difficult to believe. In it are combined such a diversity of elements, religious, magical, warlike, regal, permitting the traditional celebration of every event in human experience worthy of rejoicing or solemn ceremonial, that these occasions become heightened in our eyes, and we can say of them, as Gray said of the sunrise, 'I wonder whether anybody ever saw it before? I hardly believe it.' Although it may be a misjudgment to single out one element as more valuable than the others, the deep wounds of our civilization may be an excuse for the feeling, of passing significance, that the happiness, the gaiety, the music, and the laughter of celebrations are vital to our present needs. They have sat close to the heart of our world for many centuries. 'In the feast of Christmas,' said Stow, 'there was in the King's House, wheresoever he lodged, a Lord of Misrule or Master of merry disports.' In Scotland these mock-monarchs were known as Abbots of Unreason. They were not easily suppressed, even by a special act of Parliament, passed in 1555. In the reign of Henry VIII six members of the Privy Council signed an order for a fool's coat. And when the jesters had passed away there remained the Master of the Revels as official proof of the place of the festivities of pleasure in our national life. No one would wish this office to be revived, to add to our impersonal, bleak, and mechanized pleasures. But people can still laugh in the warmth of the sun. With the help of music and the dance they may yet remember how to celebrate splendid occasions.